The
COLOR
of
TOGETHER

MIXED METAPHORS
OF CONNECTEDNESS

The
COLOR
of
TOGETHER

MIXED METAPHORS
OF CONNECTEDNESS

MILTON BRASHER-CUNNINGHAM

Light Messages

Durham, NC

The Color of Together: Mixed Metaphors of Connectedness
Milton Brasher-Cunningham
donteatalone.com
books@lightmessages.com

Published 2020, by Light Messages
www.lightmessages.com
Durham, NC 27713 USA
SAN: 920-9298

Paperback ISBN: 978-1-61153-270-8
E-book ISBN: 978-1-61153-269-2
Library of Congress Control Number: 2020939988

for Ginger

CONTENTS

"My God, my God, thou art a direct God, may I not say a literal God, a God that wouldst be understood literally and according to the plain sense of all thou sayest, but thou art also... thou art a figurative, a metaphorical God too, a God in whose words there is such a height of figures, such voyages, such peregrinations to fetch remote and precious metaphors, such extensions, such spreadings, such curtains of allegories, such third heavens of hyperboles, so harmonious elocutions, so retired and so reserved expressions, so commanding persuasions, so persuading commandments, such sinews even in thy milk, and such things in thy words, as all profane authors seem of the seed of the serpent that creeps, thou art the Dove that flies."

–John Donne,
Devotions 1624

"I didn't need to understand the hypostatic unity of the Trinity; I just needed to turn my life over to whoever came up with redwood trees."

–Anne Lamott,
Plan B: Further Thoughts on Faith, 2006

MIXING METAPHORS

YOUR FATHER HAS HAD A STROKE. *We are on our way to the hospital.*

The text message came from my mother, just as I was finishing a worship service at a youth camp in the mountains of Arkansas. The next morning, as we prepared to leave, I looked at my friend Darren, who was the youth minister at the church, and said, "I have to go and say goodbye to my father," as though I understood what I was saying.

The next few weeks moved both quickly and in slow motion. I came down the mountain and went to the barren and boiling expanse that is Waco, Texas, where my parents lived. Dad was himself, except he sounded like some strange creature had taken control of his voice box. I went home to North Carolina, and Dad moved to rehab. Within two weeks, I was back in Texas because he had taken another turn. Looking back, I think he had a stroke no one detected. Within another fortnight, we moved from rehab to hospice to funeral, and before long, back to the routines of life that left my mother, my brother, and me in three different cities.

After the funeral, my first inclination was to call my friends whose fathers had died before mine, and say, *I'm sorry. I meant well. I had no idea this is what it felt like.* I understood something I had not before: though the weight and depth of grief felt new to me, they were not new. I had seen them in others, but I had not been able to understand. Now I did. I thought the sorrow I felt was reserved for those who had known a parent-child relationship that was a lifetime of joy, and not those for those of us who had endured periods of struggle and distance. I felt lost. I went looking for words to name the absence I had not felt before. I read any account I could find of someone's journey with grief. I wanted metaphors for the ache that I felt. I wanted stories. I wanted specifics. I wanted to know I was not alone.

John Berger wrote about going into the studio of a friend after his funeral: "The studio seemed to be like a bakery, the ovens still warm, from which the baker had just walked out to go down to the river."

Dad's absence had a presence, an aroma, a sense of who was missing.

> Missing (adj.): absent from a place, especially home, and of unknown whereabouts.

Though I can remember his voice and his laugh—I still hear them—I can't talk to him about baseball, or books, or his lunch at The Real Deal, his favorite restaurant in Waco, Texas. He is not here, and I don't know where they have taken him.

The books I did not find helpful were those that described how to get over the grief, as if it were an obstacle. Somehow I knew that grief was not something I was going to conquer or shed like a bad habit. My friend Patty, whose parents died many years before mine, told me grief was "something we learn to move around in." That made sense. I was going to live the rest of my life without my dad. I was going to live the rest of my life moving around in grief. Whatever else happened, that circumstance would not change. What could change was my perspective. I am stating the obvious, I suppose, when I say experiences of grief alter the way we look at life. When we lose the people we love—or the places, jobs, hopes—we have to look at life differently because life *is* different. There is a before and an after. The world is not the same, so we can no longer look at it in the same way.

Life with my father was not perfect. We lived through several stretches where it was difficult for both of us. I was his namesake, which often made things even more complicated. When we were living in Boston, I went back to Baylor University for Homecoming and learned that my father had preached that day on campus. I did not hear the sermon, but a friend told me that he had used me as an illustration. My father said, "In life you have to learn the difference between a problem and a predicament. A problem you can fix. A predicament is something you have to learn to live with." He paused. "I used to think my eldest son was a problem. Now I see he is a predicament."

I told that story at his funeral, and then I said, "I learned he was a predicament, too."

We had worked hard to learn to live with and love each other as we were, which was a good thing. While we were both still alive, we found a rhythm that let us both be ourselves and be together. After his death, that connection meant my ongoing predicament was that I was not going to get over missing him. And I didn't want to.

The stories of learning to live with grief that have mattered to me have honored the absence. I have listened hard to the personal accounts that made room for resonance. Their voices sang the ancient melody I could feel aching in my heart. Though what I was feeling was unfamiliar, the books I read and the conversations I had made me realize I was walking well-travelled roads, which was both comforting and disquieting. I had landed on populated shores. I had not discovered anything new.

Like many of us, as a kid I was told that in 1492, Columbus sailed the ocean blue and discovered America. He may have made the voyage, and even found a land that was not on his map, but the verb is wrong. He did not find a place that no one else had seen; he landed on a populated shore. He landed in the middle of someone else's story. He set foot where people had lived for generations, where cultures and kingdoms had already come and gone. He learned. He found, perhaps. He became aware of. He explored. He condescended. But he didn't discover a thing.

Neither have I, other than to say that in the course of my life I have discovered some things about myself, though most of those were already apparent to people around me, so even here my choice of verb is tenuous. More often than not, I feel like Mark, Ray Kinsella's brother-in-law in the movie *Field of Dreams*, who was fiercely opposed to Ray's plowing under his corn to build the baseball diamond on his farm, until he saw Doc Graham step off the field to save his niece's life. All of a sudden, where he had once seen nothing but an empty ball field, he saw a diamond teeming with players.

Not many months passed before I relinquished my title as the last of those I knew whose father had died, and I became one of those a little farther down the road. I sat with a newly fatherless friend over coffee and talked about a metaphor I had found meaningful.

"I'm learning that grief is a primary color," I said. "It's not something other than life; it is at the core of it all."

What I had begun to see was that I had known grief most all of my life because I had known loss and change on a consistent basis. I have spent a great deal of my life moving. I had lost cities and schools, friends and sacred places. What I had not known before was what it felt like for my father to die, and with him, all the things done and left undone which were a part of what it meant to be a son and to be part of a family.

My friend Doug held my words for a few moments and replied, "Then grief is not black. The three primary colors are red, yellow, and blue."

"Metaphor," Joe Moran says, "is how we nail the jelly of reality to the wall"—a statement that carries images of its own.

I learned from a different book by John Berger that the Greek word for metaphor means *porter*, as in the person on the train who helps you get from one place to another, which "is a reminder of how deeply the act of transporting, of dispatch and delivery, is intrinsic to the imagination." We spend our lives going from here to there and back again, both literally and metaphorically, and with us go the things we carry.

When Doug mentioned the three primary colors, his words expanded where the metaphor could take me. One of those places, thanks to the faith I carry, took me on an imaginative trek to the primary relationships of the Trinity, another metaphorical trio.

My seminary pastorate was a small church in the rolling hills of Coryell County of Central Texas, called Pecan Grove Baptist Church. We celebrated the church's centennial while I was there. Over that century, every one of their pastors had been a rookie. They saw their mission as helping pastors get off to a good start.

Soon after I started, I was ordained, which is what you have to do as a minister to be able to serve communion. At my ordination council—a gathering of those already ordained as both ministers and deacons to make sure the candidate is worthy—someone in the circle asked, "How do you explain the Trinity?"

"If I could do that, I'd write a book," I said.

Everyone laughed, and we went on to the next question. I suppose I can go back now and say, "Here is the book," even though I'm not trying to explain anything. But I am searching to see where the metaphor takes me, because that is what the

Trinity, like all of our names for God, is: a metaphor. A word picture that offers us a ticket to move farther down the line.

Whatever we might say about the Trinity—God in three Persons, as the hymn goes—I am captured by the picture of God as the essence of relationship. I am not writing a treatise to assign some sort of hierarchy or defend a doctrine. Early Christian theologians (mostly male) articulated their theology of the Trinity to attempt to come to terms with a God who was a cosmic mystery: Father, Son, Holy Ghost; Creator, Christ, Spirit; Maker, Redeemer, Friend. The names reflect the limitations of those trying to do the naming. Churches have split, wars have been fought, and people have been killed because metaphor was truncated into explanation. Too often, the Church is fixated on explanation—doctrine—as though the purpose of theology is orthodoxy, and the purpose of orthodoxy is compliance and conformity. The purpose of relationship, on the other hand, is intimacy, knowledge, and trust. Just being together.

One of the simplest lessons to draw from the Trinity is that life is not binary. We, as Americans, are most comfortable in a binary, polarized society. We have become accustomed to seeing most everything as either/or: Democrat or Republican, male or female, black or white, pro-life or pro-choice, Christian or Muslim, good or evil. Living at the poles handicaps the hope of relationship, because relationships are not binary, even when between two people. There is no nuance in either/or, no hope in *pick a side*. To say Jesus is the only way is not only something Jesus did not say, but also assumes life boils down to the Right Way and the Wrong Way. I am a Christian, but that does not mean I automatically assume that how I understand what it means to be in relationship with God is the only way it can happen. It also doesn't mean that I think all religions are asking the same questions.

In writing this book, I was surprised that I found myself pulled by so many Bible stories. As I went back to them, I found things I had not seen before because I was reading with eyes much more acquainted with grief. I found a collection of grief stories, which is another way of saying I found a collection of stories about relationships rather than accounts that spelled out what we are supposed to believe. Many of the writers who offered meaningful conversations with me were not people who appear to profess a faith that looks anything like mine, and yet I found resonance in their questions and observations.

Fundamentalism of any kind relies on the limited vocabulary of fear that grows out of the basic binary of Us versus Them. And we are the Ones Who Are Right. That kind of blanket coverage leaves no room for relationship because everything can be explained. It also leaves no room for metaphor because we think we have nowhere to go; we have arrived at the Truth.

Henri Nouwen described compassion as voluntarily entering another's pain. Could we then say that love is volitional inconvenience? That makes sense to me as a way to describe God, who is love. All of creation is an act of intentional inconvenience— not an expression of efficiency, or even proficiency; not a show of force as much as an invitation to wonder; artistic, yes, but not an experiment in self-promotion. Creation is a holy tangle of relationships. We continue to learn of connections we did not realize were there, or find ones that inadvertently developed. Relationships are inconvenient. Families are inconvenient. So are friendships. Join a church and see how convenient that is. Sometimes strangers seem to be the easiest to engage because we can bounce off one another like billiard balls and limit our inconvenience to passing by.

Love is inconvenient. Jesus made his ministry incredibly inconvenient by choosing disciples. How much easier it would have been if he had just called everyone to a life of fundamentalism: line up, follow the rules, don't ask questions. Instead, he loved them. He loved Mary, his mother, even as he grew into a man she often misunderstood. He loved Lazarus, and wept when he died. He loved Mary and Martha, who offered him a place that felt like home. He loved Peter and Judas.

The Trinity, as metaphor for our God, who is love, is inconvenient, which also means it is unexplainable. How much more convenient theology would be if the roles were well-defined, or if the point actually was to define the roles. Our concept of the Trinity is an attempt to find words to describe the Creator, who continues to speak the universe into existence; the Spirit infuses everything, and the Word became flesh. Any image we use comes up short of the mystery; the best we can do is to say God is Love.

The Trinity offers an image of God as relationship—a harmonizing God, a waltzing God, a multi-colored God, a God whose very nature is community. God is a holy predicament. To say, then, that we are created in the image of God is to say we are made for each other, inextricably connected, and swirled together like the colors of a painter's palette. We are all in this together; together we incarnate the image of our God.

The pages that follow are a mix of metaphors, starting with colors and moving through music, punctuation, and dinner time—all things that are essential parts of what make up my life. Conventional wisdom says we are not supposed to mix metaphors. That is good advice for an essay, I suppose. It's even advice I gave as an English teacher. Life, however, is a mixed metaphor, and a mix of them. So is faith. The language we use to talk about God and ourselves strains to carry the weight of all that matters, and so we are left with metaphors to help us make the journey.

Philosopher Max Black said a metaphor does not so much compare something to something else as much as alter what both things mean. I hope that is true. I hope we will keep adding porters, mixing our metaphors, telling our stories, and offering each other new ways of seeing.

THE COLOR
OF TOGETHER

THE COLOR OF TOGETHER

SOMETIME AFTER WE MOVED TO BOSTON, Ginger, my wife, signed me up for a watercolor class at the Boston Center for Adult Education. Our first task was to make a color wheel. We set the three primary colors—red, blue, and yellow—equidistant from each other around a circle we had drawn on the paper, and then began mixing them to show the shades it took to move from one to the other. The purples, greens, and oranges that filled in the circle illustrated the relationships between the primaries, which stood in such contrast to one another on their own. Wherever we started on the wheel, there was a connection, a way to get to the other colors.

Color is more than pigment. It is figment as well. For us to see color requires an act of imagination and an understanding of relationship.

One Christmas after the watercolors, Ginger enrolled me in an iconography class at Andover Newton Theological School. I spent over a year learning the spiritual practice from a wonderful man named Christopher Gosey. Before we ever picked up a brush, we learned the vocabulary connected to what we were doing. We were not going to paint the icons, Chris said, we were going to write them.

As one who has learned to play with words more easily than with paint, the verb choice caught me. Good writing is descriptive and evocative. The challenge is to show, not tell; to reveal. Good writing tells a story, takes us on a journey, connects us to something larger.

The "cartoons"—the outlines of the figures we would write—had been passed down for centuries, much like basic plot structures in literature, or the elements of grammar and style. The point of our work was to be faithful to those who had gone before and to what they had handed down, rather than to try and be original. Our offering was to trace the lines others had made and then color them with pigments we had mixed not so we could worship the icon, but so we could open a "window to heaven" to create a *"thin place"* for connection to God.

The phrase *thin place* entered our vocabulary through the earthy spirituality of Celtic Christianity. It describes the places where the border between what is seen and what is unseen becomes permeable. Liminal. Thin. Translucent. Transcendent. It is a sacred space of disquietude; a turbulent silence where things are still and vibrant in the same moment.

As I sat in the sun-drenched room of the aging building, listening to recordings of Russian church bells, and learning how to write my brush across the blank parchment-covered block etched with the image of Mary, I came to understand more of what Jesus meant when he said, "Lose your life to find it."

Our paint was almost translucent, by design. We mixed our colors by adding natural pigments to acrylic medium. In ancient days, the pigments were blended with egg yolks. The practice of iconography is more about prayer than painting; the necessary repetition was meditative and focusing. As we laid down the colors, we moved from heavier shades to lighter ones, choreography that held intentional theological significance. The first strokes of the lighter colors on the deep background didn't seem to have much effect, yet, over time, and with intentional repetition, the colors took hold. The deeper tones became the background—the foundation—for the illuminating presence. Without the contrast, the light would have had little significance. The base substances from which the pigments came were earthy and natural. The black was made from ashes. Some of the browns were made of dirt or powdered stone. At every level, the experience rubbed heaven and earth against each other like sticks to start a fire.

The work of icon writing is deliberate. To get a color to show up on the icon meant going over each line twenty to forty times. The spiritual practice was to turn the repetition into ritual—a sort of physical prayer. The move from heavier tones to lighter ones felt counterintuitive until I began to see the colors dawn on the icon. We traced images that had been handed down across centuries, much like we repeat rituals in worship. Everything about it was fraught with a sense of connectedness, a new way of seeing who we were in the context of who had come before and who would follow. The whole enterprise was steeped in metaphor.

In his letter to the Ephesian church, Paul wrote, "We are God's work of art, created in Christ Jesus for the good works which God has already designated to make up our way of life."[1] In a sermon on that verse, Ginger said, "We are dust, which becomes pigment in God's artwork." The pigments we used to write icons were made from earthy substances, just as we are. The Greek word translated as *work of art* is *poiema*, which even my spell check knows is the root word of poem. Paul said, "We are God's work of art." Not works. Work. Not I. We. Together we

---

1   Ephesians 2:10, NJB

become the artwork, handmade pigments illuminated by God's presence, as it has been from the dawn of creation.

Riding the color metaphor train took me to the field of the philosophy of color, which is as esoteric as it sounds, and perhaps, not a journey everyone wants to make. But I took a trip, nonetheless, as I wondered about grief as a primary color.

Philosophers look at the way humans see color, or whether we actually see color at all. One of the ways of seeing is called *color adverbialism*, which is to say, we do not see red, as much as we see red-ly. What that means is there is a relationship between the object, the perceiver, and the context—another relational trinity. The philosopher articulating the theory was not being intentionally metaphorical when she said, "Color vision is as a way of seeing things—flowers, tables, ladybirds—not, in the first instance, a way of seeing the colors." What I heard her say was the colors we see have to be connected to something or someone for them to be significant.

In 2020, our sense of what it means to be together has been heavily shaded by the COVID-19 pandemic. We have lived in quarantine, without the ability to gather, to hug those we love, to share a meal, to go to a baseball game, or to share a pew at church. I have watched people gather on the Guilford Green in groups of four or five, separating their lawn chairs to an appropriate distance just to be together. As Zoom has begun to feel like a necessary appliance in our lives, we have found ways to change backgrounds so we are surrounded by palm trees and superheroes in our little square on the screen. We are colored by our losses in ways our world has not known so pervasively for over a century.

Life, however, is a litany of losses in any age: failures, injuries, disappointments, betrayals, missed moments, things done and left undone, deaths, falls, illnesses, fears, lowered expectations. Life is also a compendium of blessings, of things for which we can be thankful: families, ball games, good food, starry nights, first kisses and last ones, friends, sunshine, spring rains, puppies, and pie. And life is an abundance of grace, of those things we stumble into, that find us, that surprise us and ambush us with the reminder of a relentless love that will not let us go. All three are true all the time. Though we often feel them singularly because of our limitations, one is not there without the others. They are the primary colors we see in the context of relationships, with something or someone, in any moment.

When we see grief-ly, grateful-ly, and grace-ly, we can see the color of together.

SEEING GRIEF-LY

Two HOURS AFTER MY FATHER DIED, we had to put Gracie, one of our Schnauzers, to sleep. I was in Waco, Texas, with my father. Ginger was in Durham, North Carolina, with our beloved pup, who had been a self-trained service dog for my father-in-law, Reuben, who had died twenty months earlier after a long battle with Alzheimer's Disease. Lola, Gracie's big sister, died a couple months after Reuben. In the years since my father's death, my mother died, we sold our favorite house, we moved from our beloved Durham, and I shut down a burgeoning cookie business, which was one of the most enjoyable things I have ever done.

But there is more to the story than what it felt like to lose three parents, two dogs, a house, a city, and a cookie cart in four years. Even though life is about what—and who—comes and goes, the story of life is about more than sorrow. The grace that comes from the relational swirls of our lives is just as quotidian and just as dependable as the grief, which means, perhaps, that responding with gratitude is the most human thing we can do in the midst of it all.

The spring before my mother died, we began to end our days in Durham. Ginger started a conversation with a church in Guilford, Connecticut, about the possibility of her pastoring there. By July, we knew we were moving, though we didn't leave until the first of November, which meant we had time to say goodbye, to see the people we wanted and needed to see, and to cram in as many of our traditional Thursday night dinners on our big front porch as we possibly could.

Our friends and our church sent us off well. The church threw a wonderful farewell dinner and dance, and then, the night before we were to drive out of Durham, a bunch of friends surprised me with a party that remains an indelible memory.

Our plan was to get up on Sunday morning, pack what was left into our Jeep Liberty, and hit the road. Packing up the house had been my primary task for several weeks, and I thought I had done a good job, especially in the kitchen, which was my domain. But when we got up that morning, it felt as though what was left in the house had multiplied. The movers had come and gone the day before, so we had only the space in our car and there was lots of stuff.

Our friend Jenny called to see if we needed help. When she arrived and saw the state of things, she began calling other friends. I walked into the kitchen and realized I had packed hardly any of it, even though I had filled boxes. Food was still in the fridge and the freezer. The cabinets were full of pretty much everything. I had blocked out the room that mattered most to me. Our kitchen was emblematic of my life in Durham, and I had no idea how to leave it. Our friends packed furiously and then divided up what could be eaten or used. We rented a U-Haul trailer to hold the things that would not fit in the car.

Ginger and I pulled out of the driveway several hours later than we had imagined, exhausted and teary. We left part of our hearts in that house and with those people, our friends who stood on our porch in tears as we drove away. They were left standing on the porch of a house of loved ones who were now absent. I have often tried to imagine how long they stood there and what they did next.

To grieve is to come to terms with an absence: something or someone being lost, or dead, or over. Life was once a certain way, and now it is not. Life has changed, and so we are changed. We must learn to live without.

How then should we live? Our responses to grief are just that: responses, rather than stages—things to move around in rather than to check off or get over. Like wood that has been stained, we are indelibly colored by grief. The pigment gets into the core of our beings.

In one of the episodes of the television show *This Is Us*, Sylvester Stallone, who played himself, says to Kevin, who was deflecting the grief of his father's death by saying it was a long time ago, "In my experience, Kevin, there's no such thing as a long time ago. There's only memories that mean something and memories that don't." Grief is living with memories that matter.

My mother went into the hospital for the last time on Christmas Day 2015. She entered hospice as the new year began and was there for thirteen days before she died. She was aware and lucid for eleven of them, welcoming friends, carrying on conversations, and getting a sense of her own ending.

When she first entered hospice, she asked her doctor, "What must I do if my goal is heaven."

The doctor dropped his head with a smile, and chuckled. "Stop eating and drinking," he said.

The morning of her eighty-fourth birthday, she took his words to heart—after taking two bites of her birthday cake—and she died three days later. The last two days, she mostly slept and did not see visitors. She died on a Friday afternoon, January 15, 2016, around five o'clock. My brother, Miller, his wife, Ginger, and I were in the room. (My brother and I are both married to women named Ginger.) We had been singing hymns, as we had done most of the afternoons in hospice. The memory of that day is clear in my mind, though I am not sure things happened in the exact order I remember them.

My brother and I sat on either side of the bed, which was the first time the two of us had done so while my mother was in hospice. We each took one of her hands. My sister-in-law was at the foot of the bed.

My brother said, "Mom, I love you," and I said the same thing.

Then he looked across the bed at me and said, "And I love you, too."

"I love you," I said. I turned to my sister-in-law, Ginger, and said, "And I love you."

As I finished my sentence, my mother stopped breathing. We could feel her leave the room.

"I think she's gone," Miller said, and we called for the nurse.

If I were writing a scene for a movie, I could not have scripted a more meaningful moment. Though it was a beautiful ending to her life, it was not different from our leaving Durham. There was still a trail of life behind her. Feelings. Details. Consequences. Beginnings. There was all kind of evidence of who she was and what she had done, but she was not there. In her place was absence.

We are all born in the middle of the story, and we will all exit before the story is finished. Countless curtain calls that make up the scope of human history, played on stages large and small, and none of them has the luxury of being the last word.

Our not being in Durham set the stage for our new chapter in Guilford. It has also called on us to find new ways to tell the stories of friendships that continue across the miles—to see things in the light of loss, much like the colors of a landscape deepen as the sun sets. That I know what it feels like to be a motherless—and fatherless—child a long way from home is the first sentence of a story I am still learning to tell.

Seeing grief-ly is coming to terms with transitions that are more complex than saying every ending is a beginning, however true that statement might be. The color of grief, of life filled with absences, is a mix of pain and possibility, of hope and loss, of love and dreams. We live in the presence of what is no longer here.

During the weeks of the COVID-19 shutdown, the absence of the lives we were used to living was palpable for many. Births, birthdays, weddings, anniversaries, deaths, and funerals were postponed, or happened in isolation. The physical presence of connecting in person proved too risky. School children went without school, but also without food. We lost the sense of who we thought we were. We lost our bearings such that we could hardly remember what day it was. The church bells rang the hour and reminded us of all that was absent.

"Teach us to number our days so we can have a wise heart."[2] I have always imagined the Psalmist who wrote those words as the Hebrew equivalent of Mr. Keating from *Dead Poets Society* calling us to seize the day, to grasp the brevity of life and understand that our days hold incredible significance. We must play as though we have no discards. The New Revised Standard Version of the Bible translates the sentence as "teach us to count our days." The difference in word choice is significant to me. To count our days feels like we are keeping score or meeting a requirement. To say we number our days is to say they add up to something.

In the mashup of midnights and cups of coffee, the days do more than roll by. They matter. And much depends on how well we pay attention to the time we have. As one of the characters in Paul Bowles's novel *The Sheltering Sky* says:

> Death is always on the way, but the fact that you don't know when it will arrive seems to take

---

2   Psalm 90:12, Common English Bible

away from the finiteness of life. It's that terrible precision that we hate so much. But because we don't know, we get to think of life as an inexhaustible well. Yet everything happens a certain number of times, and a very small number, really. How many more times will you remember a certain afternoon of your childhood, some afternoon that's so deeply a part of your being that you can't even conceive of your life without it? Perhaps four or five times more. Perhaps not even. How many more times will you watch the full moon rise? Perhaps twenty. And yet it all seems limitless.

Life moves from grief to grief, offering us the chance to number our days in sacred ways. The stones of memory stack up on certain days on my calendar, and call me to tell the stories again and remember. My father died on August 3rd, so the third day of the month has become an altar in my heart. I don't remember his death as much as his life and our life together. I mark every Opening Day of baseball season by remembering my friend David Gentiles, who shared my love of green diamonds and hopeless causes. The fifteenth of the month is a marker because of my mother. With every loss, I learn again how to number my days.

As I hear the Psalmist call us to grasp the brevity and significance of the life we have, it seems most of our numbering happens in hindsight.

Many years ago, I received a newsletter from Madeleine L'Engle that began with news of her husband's death: "He became sick at Epiphany and died just before Pentecost." The words she used to mark time feel much different than saying he got sick in January and died in May. The language of both love and liturgy call us to number our days in relationships.

W. S. Merwin has a poem called "On the Anniversary of My Death," in which he talks about marking an anniversary that has not yet been scheduled. Any day could be that day. We mostly see what the days mean as we reflect on and remember them— as we see grief-ly. Only after someone has died do we attach significance to the last time we saw them. For the most part, we don't get to see that moment coming. The absence allows us to understand the deep ritual that fed us in what once was just daily routine. Sometimes what happens in a moment renumbers the days that came before, and we see them in a new light. The death of our parents helped me and my brother find each other in new ways that continue to feed us both.

In her book *Walking on Water*, L'Engle tells the story of a village who lost track of time when their clockmaker died. Since no one was there to repair the clocks, most people abandoned their timepieces. When a new clockmaker came to town some years later, he announced that he could only repair clocks that had continued to be wound because they were the only ones that remembered how to keep time. She continues:

> So we must daily keep things wound. that is, we must pray when prayer seems dry as dust; we must write when we are physically tired, when our hearts heave, when our bodies are in pain.... We may not be able to make our 'clock' run correctly, but at least we can keep it wound, so that it will not forget.

The experiences of my life open my eyes to see that the word *wound* means one thing when it is connected to clocks, and another when it describes how we hurt. How we pronounce *wound* changes what it means. Alone on the page, without context, it could go either way. The two meanings are more connected than contradictory. The daily rituals that keep our clocks wound and mark time are often colored by the wounds with which we live.

The grief that has played out over the last several years for our family happened one day—one memory—at a time. My years on the planet have happened in days, even in moments, that have layered one on the other to create a lifetime, and there are wounds in most every layer. In yours, too. Remembering is a way of numbering our days, of adding them up, rather than separating ourselves from the past. We do not live in a straight line. The memories that feel long ago are simply those we have not wound into our present tense. They are the stories we have stopped telling.

One way to read the Bible is as a remembered collection of grief stories. I had not read them that way until my dad died. Since then, almost everyone has felt full of grief. So many of the scenes of scripture have to do with losses or deaths. And then there are the gaps in stories where we don't know what happened. In the infancy narratives of Jesus, for example, we see Mary and Joseph in the temple with Jesus when he is twelve years old. But when Jesus appeared to start his earthly ministry at thirty-three, Joseph was gone and we are not told what happened to him. My father's death let me see grief-ly enough to wonder whether Joseph's absence was a precipitating factor in Jesus' beginning his public ministry instead of staying in the carpenter's shop. We don't know, other than to see that perhaps Jesus was a person without a father when he said, "Blessed are they that mourn, for they will be comforted."

After my father died, I began to see what is commonly known as the *feeding of the five thousand,* as a story of grief. The account in Matthew's gospel, chapter 14, begins with the story of John the Baptist's capricious execution at the hand of King Herod. Jesus was heartbroken when he heard the news, and made several attempts to get away by himself to grieve over the course of the day. The disciples were relentlessly clueless. The hungry crowd kept following, until all of them were out in the middle of nowhere and the day was fading. Then the disciples told Jesus he needed to tell the people to take a dinner break.

"You give them something to eat," Jesus said. Matthew offers no indication of the tone of Jesus' voice. I hear exhaustion: *I'm tapped out. Deal with it. Please.*

"We have nothing but a little bread and some fish." The crowd was needy, the disciples were frustrated, and Jesus was grieving.

"Give me what you have," he said.

Something in the interchange reconnected Jesus to the field full of people, who were worn out as well, so he told everyone to sit, he blessed the bread and the fish, and everyone ate and shared so much that there were leftovers.

The story of humanity is a collection of grief stories. We are a community of walking wounded learning how to keep going, ending after ending.

"In the year that King Uzziah died," the prophet Isaiah wrote, "I saw the Lord." Something about the death of the king made the prophet see grief-ly. He saw God in ways he had not before, which changed the way he saw himself and those around him, perhaps the way many were changed by September 11, 2001, or the way that we will one day look back on 2020.

The stories of the Bible remain relevant because we can find ourselves in their lives and losses. They are not stories of avoidance, but of engagement. I can think of a number of people I love who are hurting deeply. Some have walked wounded for many years. Some have lost traveling companions—spouses, parents, friends, siblings. Some are reeling from pain so fresh that they are hard to reach. The best I can do is wait for them. I look up and beyond those close to me and see concentric circles of grief that reach around the globe and across time. Some days it feels like there is so much pain and hunger for healing, and all we have is the spiritual equivalent of a little boy's sack lunch to offer in return.

One of the places I learn about living and dying is in the garden behind our barn, a 50-by-40-foot communal plot that I help tend alongside a group of church members. The reality of agriculture is that things have to die for other things to live—and for others to eat. I have spent many a spring and summer morning killing squash bugs so the zucchini could thrive. The Mexican bean beetle, a creature that looks like a wrong-colored ladybug, lays eggs on the underside of the zucchini leaves that hatch into small yellow worms. Some mornings I have squashed fifty or sixty of them, leaving both my fingers and the leaves stained yellow. If the bugs die, the squash lives. The reverse is also true. The ravaged plants in early summer, and the fading garden in the fall, speak to both life and finiteness.

Theologian Maggi Dawn talks about the early Christians' sense of "passing through" not being escapist as much as purposeful: their earthly lives mattered because they were temporary. We often act as though our institutions are what provide permanence, but that notion is counter-divine because it offers a false sense of stability and respectability and accomplishment—a false sense of eternity. No matter how big our cathedrals or capitols, it's all going the way of the squash bugs and the zucchini leaves.

We are all living grief stories of days that are numbered, and sorrows that can nourish when we are willing to share them.

SEEING GRACE-LY

MY BROTHER, MILLER, AND I often have differing political opinions. Our discussions are energetic without getting contentious, and we rarely solve anything or change one another's minds. In the middle of one such discussion, he repeated a phrase he had learned: "Whoever frames the question wins the argument."

I continue to be intrigued by his choice of verb: *frame*. To frame something is to set the parameters, to contextualize, to define the field of vision, whether we are talking about a painting, a picture, a debate, or a theological perspective.

Director Martin Scorsese said, "Cinema is a matter of what's in the frame and what's out," which is to say, how we set boundaries matters.

When my friend Terry has to call a company's customer service line, he frames the conversation by saying, "I am calling because I have a problem. Are you the person who can help me, or do I need to talk to someone else?" His framing question creates an ally on the other end of the line, regardless of how they answer. A frame, in one way or another, says, *Look at it this way*.

For much of Christian history, the frame through which we have chosen to see humanity has been the Fall, which is the stained-glass name for Adam and Eve's choice to bring sin into the world, thus making all of their descendants sinful. The frame of such a theology starts the story of humanity by saying we are damaged goods. We are hopeless causes. Our sin is an indelible mark responsible for all the pain in the world, and all the death as well. In this frame, Jesus had to be killed because we are so tainted with sin that we could only be saved by his sacrificial blood. He paid our debt because we are liabilities to God, not assets.

But to start the story with sin misses a larger, more essential frame. In the beginning, God created the universe and saw that it was good—including us. Grace is the first frame intended to set our vision, not sin. We are wonderfully and uniquely created in the image of God, and worthy to be loved. Grace is the color in God's palette that gets laid down first. Grief may go back as far as the stories go, but grace is there before any story begins. Grace is the framing narrative, whether it is the grace of a moonrise or a sunset, the grace of the changing tides, the grace of one breath and then another. Whatever the picture, whatever the color of life in any given moment, grace is not only the frame, but also the foundation. The primer.

I am not saying that everything will always turn out well on a situational level. I'm not saying that sin is not a reality, or that the consequences of sin do not have profound effects on our lives. I am saying that from the first word that spoke us into existence, we are loved and we are not alone. Our lives are marked by a belonging we have not earned, even when we can't feel it. We may be broken, but we are not worthless. We are worthy of loving and being loved.

Both grief and grace are received more than they are created, demanded, or deserved. Grace meets us at every turn, in everything from giggling children to falling leaves, should we choose to see grace-ly. It is grace that calls us into our grief in a way that leads us to gratitude.

As much as life is full of difficult things, it is also shot through with grace—unearned moments where we are reminded that we matter, that we belong, that we are connected. We are here to help each other create those moments, hear those words. We can't see them by ourselves. We must help each other ask good questions. How we make meaning is in the questions we ask, and perhaps, the tone in which we ask them.

One of my favorite Q&A scenes in scripture is between God and the prophet Elijah, who was hiding in a cave out of fear and self-pity because things had not gone as planned, to put it mildly. The queen was out to kill him. Elijah was scared and despondent and throwing a pity party in his hideout. God found him and said, "What are you doing here?" The Bible gives us no indication of tone in God's delivery. Elijah could have heard the question as an opening for relationship, or as a prelude to judgment. When the prophet stopped his pity party long enough to listen for God, God said nothing and reminded Elijah—in the "sound of sheer silence"—that he was there by grace. He came out of the cave and went down the mountain and into town, changed by the question.

Pastor and author Mike Stavlund says, "Surely, things like faith, hope, love, and salvation are good. They are, in my view, the answers we long for, and which we desperately need. But the answers are not enough—we need the questions."

He's right. We need good questions to frame our lives.

In the frame of Luke's gospel, Jesus and the disciples were working their way through a crush of humanity on their way to the house of Jarius, a religious leader whose daughter was gravely ill.

As the people crowded in against him, Jesus stopped and said, "Who touched me?"

The disciples must have laughed out loud.

"Seriously? Who touched you? We're in a crowd. Everyone touched you."

"I felt power go out of me," Jesus replied.

A woman stepped out of the crowd. She had been hemorrhaging for twelve years. Her desperation had driven her to reach for Jesus as he passed, even if just to touch the hem of his cloak. She thought the chance meeting would make a difference. In the press of people around Jesus, she thought a simple touch could change things. It did.

In the incidental contact that colors our days, how often do we feel the power of grace go out of us? How aware are we of our chance to offer compassion to someone, or to make ourselves approachable so people will feel the resonance and ask for help?

That grace is undeserved has been a hard lesson for me to learn. I am the third in the line of Miltons in my family, named for my father, who was named for his father. Why the name Milton was chosen for my grandfather is not a story my family kept telling. What I do know is that a frame of unworthiness came with the name, though both of the Miltons that preceded me handed down a better world and a better self-image than the one they were given.

Nevertheless, feeling like I was enough has not been my strong suit. I learned early that love was something earned. I thought most people—and God—wanted to know what I had done for them lately. Let me be clear: it was the lesson I learned, not necessarily the one that was taught. My parents told me they loved me every day, more than once. They said they were proud of me, though they were more general than specific. But as I watched my dad work hard to feel like he mattered, I learned to work hard, too. I learned to feel, like him, that I was never enough.

God doesn't love us out of pity or because of our proficiency. God's unearned love means we matter because we are breathing, not because we have racked up a lifetime of accomplishments. Grace means we exist in the paradox of appropriate insignificance: it matters that we are here, but no more than anyone else. In Psalm 8, the poet asked,

> When I look at your heavens, the work of your fingers
>
> the moon and the stars that you have established;
>
> what are human beings that you are mindful of them,
>
> mortals that you care for them?

and offered another case where there is more than one way to hear the question. And again, it's all about tone. "What are humans that you are mindful of them?" We can hear those words with a tone of wonder or of sarcasm. To talk about grace is to talk about the tone of God.

Tone is a color word as well as a speech word. Could it be that to hear God say, "That's good," again and again in Genesis is best heard less like an imperial pronouncement, and more like the exuberance of a child on the playground? Listen to the tone of Jesus as he stared down the judgment in the disciples' questions and the wonderings of the religious power brokers as to why he hung out with those whom the privileged considered disposable:

> Come to me, all who are weary and heavy-laden.
>
> Blessed are those that mourn, for they shall be comforted.
>
> Let the little children come to me."

We often focus on the stories of Jesus that loom large—the feeding of the five thousand, his walking on water—but the majority of the stories are small ones: individual encounters, dinners, conversations, and specific situations. When we tell the stories of our lives that matter most to us, they are full of details. They are made up of the moments when nothing else could help and love lifted us with a specific word or action. We can't last long on slogans and ideas, no matter how inspiring. We need them to become flesh and blood to really make a difference.

I am at an age where when I go to the doctor, they always say, "Have you fallen in the last six months?" They are asking a practical question, but I hear it as a metaphor, particularly since I had my right knee replaced. More than once, my surgeon cautioned me not to fall on it because I could do serious damage. But we all fall down. And we get up. Such is the rhythm of life. Yet falling is not the same as being fallen, which takes me to one my favorite passages from *The Catcher in the Rye*, where Holden Caulfield says to his sister Phoebe:

> "You know that song 'If a Body Catch a Body Comin' Through the Rye'? I'd like—"
>
> "It's 'If a body meet a body coming through the rye'!" old Phoebe said....
>
> "I thought it was 'If a body catch a body,'" I said. "Anyway, I keep picturing all these little kids playing some game in this big field of rye and all. Thousands of little kids, and nobody's around— nobody big, I mean—except me. And I'm standing on the edge of some crazy cliff. What I have to do, I have to catch everybody if they start to go over the cliff—I mean if they're running and they don't look where they're going, I have to come out from somewhere and catch them. That's all I'd do all day. I'd just be the catcher in the rye and all. I know it's crazy, but that's the only thing I'd really like to be. I know it's crazy."

Crazy, yes, in the same way our extravagantly creative God breathed us into existence and was then crazy enough to think we are all worth loving.

I grew up being taught that grace was primarily about salvation—by grace we are saved through faith—and that the point of salvation was about being taken out of this world, if you will. If I was saved, then I was going to heaven. Whether verbalized or not, the sometimes not-so-underlying message was that the point of getting saved was to get out from under the suffering caused by our sin.

There's more than one problem with the messages in that sentence. I never understood why I wanted to be saved from this life, or if I was saved in the way it was described to me, why life kept hurting. And then there was the whole bloody atonement that required Jesus to die for such a wretch like me. Salvation has to be more than an eternal escape hatch. Rebecca Solnit says:

> Saving is the wrong word, one invoked over and over again, for almost every cause. Jesus saves and so do banks; they set things aside from the flux of earthly change.... Saving suggests a laying up where neither moth not rust doth corrupt; it imagines an extraction from the dangerous, unstable, ever-changing process called life on earth. But life is never so tidy and final.

To be saved by grace is to accept God's invitation into the middle of life, as Jesus demonstrated by the way he lived. He didn't save himself. In fact, that was the very temptation he stared down again and again from the beginning of his ministry. Grace offers us the opportunity to make more of our pain, suffering, and grief than judgment, hopelessness, or despair. Grace calls us together by reminding us that the love we know, and we have to share, is both unearned and unending, which means we can share it freely. That's about as primary as it gets.

The real power of grace in our lives is not in the giant step of eternal salvation. That's settled: we belong to God. Where grace matters most is in the daily details, the quotidian encounters where we have a chance to step into the contagion that ripples through the grief of our lives, where we pass grace hand to hand to make meaning together. Maybe one of the main lessons of the Incarnation is that grace needs a face, and hands, and feet. Grace is not merely a concept; it is flesh and blood. To talk about it as unmerited favor just leaves us with a definition that requires further explanation. But when we incarnate it—when we offer our human touch—things change.

We use the word grace to talk about movement. She moves with grace. He acted gracefully. It describes a fluidity, an integration. The dancer who moves gracefully knows their body, has connected heart and limbs such that they can put emotion into motion, and draw a physical picture of how we can be in the world when we trust that we are wonderfully and uniquely made in the image of God, and worthy to be loved.

To move gracefully is to lean into muscle memory, which means it takes practice. Spiritual practice. One of the therapists I have seen in my life taught me that I could "act my way into a new way of feeling." Feelings are a response and, therefore, based in choice. My first response may seem involuntary, but I can act my way into a new response—a practiced response—and I can keep practicing until I change what feels normal.

Grace is the name for the prayer we say at dinner when we pause and realize all the connections that got us to the table. We pause to remember that we would not be here if it weren't for the unearned connections that keep reminding us that we belong. Yet they can become invisible. Circumstances can dull our vision, or even blind us to all that tethers us, and so we say grace and frame our daily lives with these questions: How am I dishing out unearned significance? How am I blocking it? What is the prevailing tone of my life?

We have to be intentional about reminding each other of the ties that catch us. We have to practice staying connected. We have to choose to do so. We have to pay attention: that's the cost of meaningful relationship. We have to come by every day and lay a fresh coat of grace for one another, offer an unearned reminder that we are all loved.

Salvation is not a cosmic gesture as much as a constellation of small actions that carry love. We are called to color the world in tones of grace. We are saved one day at a time, one day after another, together.

SEEING GRATEFUL-LY

THE YEAR BEFORE MY FATHER DIED my parents sold their home in Waco and moved into an apartment building. They were ready for less space, which meant they had a house full of stuff to go through, divide up, or get rid of. In the process of going through papers, my mother found a thank-you note I had written to my grandmother one Christmas. I was probably about ten, and I was transparent about why I was writing:

> Dear Grandma,
>
> Mom says if I don't write I won't get any more presents, so I am writing to say thank you for you what you sent.
>
> Love,
>
> Milton

My letter was indicative of obligation more than gratitude.

Early in their marriage, my brother and sister-in-law lived in Akron, Ohio. My brother's barber was a man who had come from

Lebanon as a refugee back when Lebanon was much like Syria is today. He and his family literally had to flee their country with only the clothes they were wearing, leaving behind a successful business, a home, their relatives, and their lives. In Akron, he had found work as a barber, a job that reflected neither his passion nor his training. He was doing the work he could find to survive. Miller said that any time he asked, "How are you today?" the man replied, "Grateful." He took my brother's routine question seriously and responded with something other than a summary of his circumstances.

In his first letter to the Thessalonians, the apostle Paul wrote, "Never stop praying. Be thankful, whatever the circumstances may be." The admonition was not to be thankful for every circumstance, but to be grateful in the middle of whatever was going on, which means Paul was talking about something more profound than the what-do-you-say kind of thank-you notes my mother demanded of me. The people that Paul was writing to knew little of power, prestige, or privilege, much less safety. They were acquainted with grief, persecution, and poverty. They knew that what mattered cost something. For them, it was no accident that prayer and gratitude went together. Keep praying. Keep listening. Keep saying thank you. If we lean into the grace and live in the middle of the grief, gratitude is a primary color—a primary response.

When Jesus began the Beatitudes with, "Blessed are the poor in spirit, for theirs is the kingdom of heaven," one of the things he was saying was that those who are hopeless, downtrodden, marginalized, or desperate have a better grasp of gratitude than those of us who—to paraphrase Texas politician Jim Hightower—were born on third base and think we hit a triple, the stuff we accumulate often changes our priorities. When our security becomes more valuable than solidarity, we forget how to be thankful. When we become creatures of comparison, we lose sight of what we have. When we allow ourselves to presume our privilege is deserved, we diminish our capacity for gratitude.

Much of life, it seems, can get in the way of being grateful. The barber in Akron could have chosen to be bitter about all that he had lost. He could have lashed out. He could have chosen to stay trapped in comparison with the comfortable people who came in for haircuts. Instead, he chose to say thanks whenever he got the chance.

When I think of what I learned about *thank you* growing up, the story of Jesus' encounter with the ten men who had leprosy comes to the top of my memory. Jesus was walking on the border between Samaria and Galilee, an area rife with conflict and division, and with prejudice and discrimination. The men lived on the margins of society since they were considered unclean and contagious because of their disease. But they were not contagious. Their isolation was unfounded. They cried out to Jesus for mercy. He told them to go into town and show themselves to the priest, which was the only way they could re-enter society. They ran off to do as he said. Then one—a Samaritan—came back to say thank you. Jesus said, "Where are the other nine? Is it only this foreigner who returned?"

When I learned this story as a child, the moral I heard was not unlike my mother's admonition to write thank-you notes: The one who came back to say thanks was the good guy. Don't be an ingrate like most people.

The story is not that simple.

In the early nineties, Ginger and I went to Carville, Louisiana to visit the Hansen's Disease Center just before it permanently closed. Hansen's Disease is the modern name for leprosy. Ginger had worked there for a semester between college and seminary. I remember how quiet and sacred the space felt. The buildings and the grounds that held the stories of those who had been sequestered for most of their lives felt filled with an unarticulated reverence. Most of the stories they held were never told beyond those walls. The gravestones in the cemetery were engraved with patient numbers, not names.

A treatment for Hansen's Disease was found and has allowed the one hundred twenty-five Americans a year that contract the disease to get help. But the folks who lived and died at Carville lived and died before that treatment was developed. They lived their lives cared for, but also trapped and forgotten.

In Jesus' day, those who lived with leprosy also knew a thing or two about being outcast. Their disease required that they live in isolation. The border between the antagonistic regions of Galilee and Samaria was as close as they could get to anyone else. When they called out, Jesus didn't make a big statement about healing, or say anything other than, "Go show yourselves to the priest." The priest was the only one who could declare them healed and allow them back into society. Nine of the ten followed Jesus' instructions because nine of the ten were Jews who could go see the priest. The other one, a Samaritan, knew a visit to the priest was not going to make much difference because leprosy was not the only thing that marginalized him. He had been able to be with the other nine because they were all sick and outcast. Even healed of his disease, he still would not be allowed to belong. He would continue to live at the margins. When the others went to the synagogue, he came back to say thank you.

The brevity of the gospel account offers no explanation for why the man returned. Maybe he came back to say thanks because, at least for a moment, he didn't feel trapped or forgotten. For a moment, he felt whole, human, noticed, even loved.

Luke says Jesus turned him, briefly, into an object lesson. "Did only the foreigner come back to say thanks?" he said, in what I imagine was his crowd-on-the-hillside stage whisper. But the Samaritans weren't foreigners in the land. They were not strangers to the Jews. They were the minority. The two ethnic groups had lived in perpetual proximity for generations, and had chosen to keep an intentional and familiar distance from one another.

Jesus knew a more significant barrier than the disease had been broken by the man's gratitude, and he spoke directly to him, and more intimately: "Get up. Your faith has made you well." The man had already been healed of his leprosy. Gratitude was not a requirement for that healing. The other nine didn't get to the synagogue, only to find that their leprosy had returned because they had not gone back to Jesus with a thank-you note.

Hardly anyone Jesus healed ever said thank you, according to the gospel accounts. Some went walking and leaping and praising God, but not many said thanks. Yet they all stayed healed. What, then, was made well by the man's return? His gratitude afforded him the chance to feel whole, to feel human, separate of a societal decree. He didn't need a priest to tell him he was allowed in. Perhaps, when he did get to town, and someone asked how he was, he replied, "I'm grateful."

In the middle of all that hurts in the world, of all that is wrong or unjust or painful, of all that throws us to the edges of existence, gratitude offers us the chance to be made well. In the middle of grief, our faith that grace is true—that God's love will not let us go—comes alive in gratitude.

Cateura is the largest garbage dump in Ascension, Paraguay, which is the city where Julie, our former foster daughter, was born. She was adopted as an infant and has lived all her life in Massachusetts. She lived with us while she was in high school. As an adult, she went on a Habitat build to see her birth country for the first time, and she met Favio Chavez, who, years ago, saw the children who lived in and around the dump, and began the Landfill Harmonic Orchestra to offer them music and hope. Chavez teaches the children to play, and conducts the orchestra, which now travels around the world. His work was documented in the film *Landfill Harmonic: A Symphony of the Spirit.*

The filmmakers interviewed a woman whose husband made instruments out of oil cans and other things he found in the giant trash heap. She talked about their house, their pigs and chickens, and her husband, who no longer had to work at the dump to find recyclable materials to sell. Then she said, "I don't think my life could be any better."

The nine who went into town had done as they were told. They also had a ticket back into society. Perhaps they equated their healing with things being *made right.* They had been wronged by leprosy; now they deserved their place in society. Think of all of the years they had lost. I don't know that I would have felt any different.

Being healed of leprosy was a big deal, but the man who came back to say thanks understood it was not the whole deal. He didn't deserve the healing any more than he deserved the disease. He was still stuck on the outskirts of a border town, and he didn't deserve that either. Most of his life was not going to be changed, yet what was changed by Jesus mattered enough to say thank you. Like the woman on the edge of the garbage dump, he knew it was as good as it was going to get. Like the barber in Akron, he was grateful.

The reality of my life is I have more than I need—even in the months when we have not been sure how all the bills would be paid. Even during the COVID-19 isolation, I had enough food, I didn't live alone, I was able to do my job from home and continue to receive my salary, and I had space to walk in our town, where people respected the need for physical distancing. Beyond the economics, I am a straight, white, cisgender, Christian, American male. I am a person of profound privilege. For me to understand what it means to be hopeless and desperate means I must do way more listening and learning than preaching or pontificating. It means I must learn how to play a supporting role. When I do speak, I need to speak up for someone other than myself.

What I do need is to give up being right, or being in charge, or being in control. I need to let go of assuming life will always allow me to be comfortable. I need to trust that God's grace covers me. I need to come to the table to be fed, to feel connected, and to be reminded that grief, grace, and gratitude are inextricably bound to one another relationally—and that gratitude is more than a thank-you note.

Maybe gratitude, rather than freedom, is another word for nothing left to lose. The inevitability of grief reminds us that loss in intrinsic to life. We lose something, or someone, almost every day. Grace is unstoppable and unearned, and it calls us to risk, to choose not to measure our steps, but live with hopeful abandon. Failure is inevitable as well, though not ultimate.

At one of the significant transitions in my life, of which there have been several, I did a mass mailing of my resume trying to find work and I came up with nothing. One night, Ginger said, "You fail better than anyone I know." It's still my favorite compliment. Life is painful and risky and hard, and—not but—life is filled with good things. We are made well by our gratitude; we are also made one.

David Steindl-Rast says,

> [I]f you're grateful, you're not fearful. And if you're not fearful, you're not violent. If you're grateful, you act out of a sense of enough and not from a sense of scarcity, and you're willing to share.

His progression of thought haunts me in the best way: if we are grateful, we are not fearful; if we are not fearful, we are not violent. Violence is an act of fear, not a statement of power. Though the powerful may wield the weapons, they attack out of fear. Violence is the choice of last resort. It is a thankless act. It is the harsh articulation that there is no possibility of relationship. It is a physical manifestation of despair. Though we may choose to see it, sometimes, as a justified reaction, it is not a solution. Fear is never a solution.

The alarming tenor of what passes for discourse in our country will not be changed by someone shouting louder or expressing more extreme ideas of hatred and bigotry. The level of violence in the world will not be lowered by someone dropping a bigger bomb, building bigger prisons, or erecting higher walls. Blessed are the peacemakers. Blessed are those who mourn. Blessed are the refugees. Blessed are the poor in spirit. And blessed are the grateful.

Jesus' list of blessed ones is not a catalog of the fortunate. He names those who choose not to be defined by their circumstances, but choose, instead, to act out of gratitude rather than scarcity and fear. We lose our vocabulary for gratitude when fear becomes our common vernacular. We lose the words that matter most and, as a result, we lose part of our humanity.

The Simien Mountains in Ethiopia is home to the Gelada Baboons, who get up before sunrise and climb as high as they can so they can applaud the sunrise. They start their day in gratitude. Our town of Guilford sits on the shoreline of the Long Island Sound, which faces south. Though we are on the East Coast, we can see both sunrise and sunset from our little harbor. I can't claim to have seen every one, but I have stood there enough to know that the baboons are on to something.

We live in difficult days. The tone of our political rhetoric is reducing our cultural vocabulary to one of violence, conquest, and conflict. We are being fed a steady diet of ideas that would have us believe scarcity and security are the words we must settle for: *There is not enough. Be afraid. We are under attack. Fight back. Get what's yours. Kick everyone else out.*

No. We are more than the sum of our fears. We are called to live lives colored by gratitude. Do justice. Love kindness. Walk humbly with God and with one another. Inhabit the truth that there is enough to go around by sharing, by risking, and by standing in solidarity. Stand out under the stars, or on a beach, or in the middle of your backyard and clap like a gratuitously grateful baboon, connected and caught up in the mystery that is larger than all of us.

When we are grateful, we are not fearful. To live thankfully is to live faithfully, for faith is trusting that love, not fear, will have the last word.

In the office where I work we had an internal discussion about ways to improve our daily processes to make things more efficient, and, well, easier on everyone. Email is our primary means of communication, since many of us work remotely. We all get lots of email, and a lot of it comes from each other. In the course of the discussion, one person suggested that we go back to something they had done previously, which was to not send a thank-you response when someone completed a task or answered a request. "We know we're thankful; we don't need to say it." They meant well, and their tone was not harsh, but their words saddened me. I didn't want to lose the thank yous.

In these days, or any days, a word of gratitude or praise is worth saying out loud or writing down, both to encourage and to grow the trust necessary for more difficult feedback, should the need arise. Letting the thanks go unsaid sets the stage to let other things go unsaid as well—things that need to be said, but are not said easily. Life has a centrifugal force that pulls us apart. The flow of our days, from emails to errands, from schedules to surprises, draws us away from each other, unless we choose differently. The day-to-day demands can lead us to see those around us as little more than furniture.

When Paul wrote, "Be thankful, whatever the circumstances may be," who he was calling us to thank is not specified. Thank God? Certainly. And I am not misreading the text to think he might also be calling us to a more extravagant expression of our gratitude: say thank you to whomever you can, every chance you get.

Say the words. Thank you for making the bed. Thank you for pouring my coffee. Thank you for opening the door. Thank you for filling my water glass. Thank you for doing your job. Thank you for answering my email. Thank you for picking up our trash. Thank you for doing a job I would never want to do. Thank you for showing up. Thank you for...well, just thank you. Every little gust of gratitude blows against the centrifugal force of life, pulling us closer together and offering us the chance to connect. It is not a waste of time, nor is it merely meeting an expectation or an obligation. To say thanks is to recognize our shared humanity, to relish in the resonance of being created in the image of God.

Whatever the circumstance, let us be thankful. Let us choose gratitude as our primary response to life.

Many years ago, Billy Crockett and I wrote a song called "Let Us Be Thankful Boys and Girls." I read the words now, thirty years after we wrote them, and they still ring true.

> Let us be thankful boys and girls
> when hope is not enough that death can't bury love
> for wine and bread and hymns remembering again
> we follow the beat of amazing grace
> oh let us be thankful boys and girls

One of my favorite names for communion is the Eucharist, which comes from the Greek word for thank you. The central table of Christianity is one of gratitude that grows out of memory and ritual, out of the intentional, meaningful repetition of what matters most: the Great Thanksgiving.

"As often as you do this," Jesus said, "Remember me." Remember that love is stronger than death. Remember as we have said more than once, that we are not alone. Remember that we are more than our possessions. Remember that life is about more that feeling secure. Remember that the baboons clap for the sunrise. Remember that God is still speaking. Remember that love gets the last word.

Remember. And be grateful.

SEEING TOGETHER-LY

GINGER AND I ONCE SPENT THE NIGHT in Las Vegas, just so we could say we had been there. I was walking out of the hotel one morning and happened to be behind two folks who thought it was still the night before.

One said, "There two things in life you've got to know: you've got to know where you're at, and you've got to know where you're going."

"Well, hell," said the other, "I've always knowed where I was at, but I ain't never knowed where I was going."

I told that story in a sermon once, and a friend who was much more acquainted with science than I am, sent me a note describing the Heisenberg Uncertainty Principle, which says, "No thing has a definite position, a definite trajectory, or a definite momentum. Trying to pin a thing down to one definite position will make its momentum less well-pinned down, and vice-versa," which is to say, if you focus on where a thing is, you can't keep track of how or where it is going or exactly how fast it is moving. If you focus on tracking its movement, you can't mark where it is. You can only take one of the measurements at a time. The principle comes from the study of subatomic particles called quarks.

Most of the above paragraph is beyond the reach of my knowledge. I am fascinated, however, by what little I understand of physics, mostly because its language is full of metaphor. To say we cannot measure movement and location at the same time seems as true for human beings as it does for the subatomic particles that make up our universe. Quarks are not able to exist alone. They must be in relationship if they are to survive. They also appear to communicate with each other. And they change when they are observed. Though I cannot see them, and I struggle to comprehend the science, I get the picture. And you do not have to be a quantum physicist to see where I am going. We see together-ly.

As those created in the image of God, we are built for relationship. That is the heart of what the Trinity is about. God is a quantum God, if you will, who exists in relationship, whose very essence is relationship, and we are made in God's image. We are built for conversation and compassion, made to grow and learn and change together. Whether we are standing still or moving fast, we are in this together.

The truth that both life and faith are team sports comes from both our Creator and the tiny unseen building blocks of our universe. We have to listen to the world with borrowed ears, to trust what resonates with each other. We have to lean into what can help us understand one another if we want to make meaning of our lives. We, like quarks, are not going to figure it out alone. Neither are the physicists or the theologians or the philosophers. On our own, we don't know where we are or where we are going. The picture is both too expansive and too detailed. We need each other.

I see the acres of trees that cover much of our Connecticut landscape, and they look like they are just standing there.

37

Yet thanks to Tom, a friend who loves trees, I learned they communicate through a microscopic network of fungi called mycorrhiza, which runs for miles and miles and enables them to share nutrients and take care of one another. They, like us, need each other to exist and to grow, even as their essential communication goes unseen by much of the rest of creation. We even miss that their communication is essential to our existence. The silence of the trees also gives me hope that I am not just spouting an extrovert's gospel when I say we are connected.

The writer of the Epistle to the Hebrews reminds us that "Faith means putting our full confidence in the things we hope for. It means being certain of things we cannot see"—like talking trees and invisible particles, and all that ties us together.

To talk about the color of together means that fundamentally I have to think beyond myself. I have to live beyond myself. To say that grief is a primary color is to say that it is an inevitable and essential element, and that it is one of the things that binds us together. Love is shared loss. Grace is the indelible presence of God in our lives that creates and sustains our togetherness. Gratitude calls me outside of myself because it reminds me I am not self-contained. I have been given much I had nothing to do with. I am a receiver, perhaps more than I am a giver or a creator.

How much our lives are intertwined became more apparent at almost every level of life during the COVID-19 quarantine. We were reminded that none of us can survive alone. We were also reminded that life is a beautiful temporary, as poet Brian Doyle called it, and we are here to color it together. These fleeting days matter because we share them with one another. We make lifelong promises in a world that offers few guarantees.

Our days may be fleeting, but we are not painting in temporary shades. The colors of life leave permanent marks, even as those of us who paint them fade out of the picture. We can see the color of together best when we are not looking for the future, but are committed to community in the present.

The best way we can prepare for whatever may come is to live together today.

One December, on the longest night of the year, I wrote this poem:

solstice

come sit in the dark with me
and look at that moon that
is so at home in the night
let us reach deep into the
pockets of our souls for
scraps of hope and wonder

come look up at the firefly
stars flinging their light
lay back on the blanket of
dead leaves and sleeping soil
would that we had a ladder to
make a consolation of ourselves

come sing our favorite song
softly into this silent night that
welcomes the first day of winter
the one about being together
no matter what—yes—that one
come sit in the dark with me

I intended for the last two lines of the second stanza to be:

would that we had a ladder to
make a constellation of ourselves,

as though we would all climb up into the magic of a starlit night. But my autocorrect had a mind of its own and wrote *consolation*. I posted the poem, but didn't catch the mistake until the following day as I was responding to a comment. I started to fix it, but decided to leave it alone, even though the word consolation made the ladder superfluous. Instead, I looked up the definitions of the two words to learn more about what I had written:

> *Constellation:* (noun) a group of associated or similar people or things.
>
> *Consolation:* (noun) 1.) the comfort received by a person after a loss or disappointment; 2.) a goal scored at a point when it is no longer possible for the scoring team to win.

Though I am not sure I have ever thought of the two words as connected, I found an affinity when I looked at them together. Though I thought the idea of making a constellation of ourselves was cool—a gathering together to shine—my mistake let me see that to make a consolation of ourselves feels even more significant—and I am taking both definitions into account. We are most truly human when we comfort one another. As one who lives with depression, I am grateful for those who take time to offer consolation.

However, I hear the second definition—a goal when there is no longer a chance of winning—as more profound than scoring in an already-decided contest.

In one of my favorite movies, *Miss Firecracker*, Carnelle Scott (Holly Hunter) is a woman in the last year of her eligibility for the Miss Firecracker Contest in Yazoo City, Mississippi. Her cousin Elain (Mary Steeburgen) had won it years before, and Carnelle is sure she can do the same. She places fifth. In the midst of her disappointment, she gets up to march in the parade.

Elain condescendingly suggests that she doesn't have to go, and Carnelle replies, "When you come in fifth place, you have to march behind the float."

Later, Mac Sam (Scott Glenn), the come-and-go love of her life, says to her, "I'll always remember you as the one who could take it on the chin."

Not long after, she says, "I just want to know what I can reasonably expect out of life."

> "Not much." He laughs and coughs at the same time.
>
> "But something," she replies.
>
> "Eternal grace," he says.

To lean into the second definition of consolation—the unnecessary goal—is not to say that life is a lost cause, as much as to point out that winning is not what matters most. I trust with all of my being that love is going to have the last word, and I have chimed in more than once when someone says, "Love wins." But that victory will not come about because either we or God started kicking ass and taking names. We make a consolation of ourselves not so we can win, but so we can be together.

If we expect victory out of life, most of us will come up short. If we expect love, and we go looking for it, we will make a consolation of ourselves—a true work of art.

(ONE MIC,
ONE TAKE)

PRACTICE LIFE

ONE OF THE RECURRING SCENES my father and I played out during my childhood came after he and I had had a confrontation, which usually involved some sort of discipline that was never easy for either one of us. He would circle back to make sure I understood his actions.

"You were first," he would say. "We didn't get a practice kid."

Many years later, after seeing *Dead Poets Society*, I wrote lyrics for a song called "Walking on the Earth," rephrasing Mr. Keating's call to *carpe diem*—to seize the day. One of the lines was, "There is no practice life, this is it." Though life does offer some moments that allow us a do-over, we get one shot at the day we are living. We say what we say, we do what we do, we see what and whom we see. Our current use of the word draws a distinction between practice and performance—practice as rehearsal—but at its deepest root, practice means to do, or to act. We practice life by living it.

My friend Laura introduced me to the music of a jazz singer named Gregory Abbott, and his song "Take Me to the Alley," in particular. The song is a parable about a king who responds to all the ways the wealthy in the kingdom have fixed everything up for him by asking to be taken to the alleys so he can see where the real people live. After listening to the song, I went looking for a video version and found one on YouTube, subtitled "(one mic, one take)." It was exactly that. The musicians were playing live, and Abbott stood at a mic and delivered the song in the moment. As I watched the video for the third or fourth time, it struck me: our practice life is just that: one mic, one take.

It would be an overstatement to say I am a jazz aficionado, but there is much of it that moves me. John Coltrane's *A Love Supreme* speaks a language to my heart that I don't know how to translate, but I still understand. Thelonious Monk lets me hear "Abide with Me" as so much more than a funeral hymn.

I am far from the first to think about jazz as a metaphor. There are books about running your business like jazz, thinking about life like jazz, and cooking like jazz, to name a few. One of the attractions of the metaphor is how it combines the patterns that are in place with the room to move and find new expressions.

Improvisation is one of the hallmarks of jazz, particularly when it comes to live performance. There may be more than one microphone, but it is one night, one take. It is amazing to watch three or four musicians together on stage, all sharing the familiar framework of a song, and then taking turns leading each other on serendipitous uncharted excursions of music and friendship. It's about a lot more than everyone just doing their thing. It is a tangible picture of relationship. It is listening, responding, and belonging—all of which take practice.

The main reason I don't play piano is I didn't want to. My mother signed me up for lessons when I was in first grade. After six months and three teachers, the last of them came to the car when my mom picked me up, and said, "Do us both a favor and let the boy quit." I wasn't learning to read music because I could hear what my teacher was playing and repeat it. She caught me by intentionally playing notes that were not on the page, and I played them as well. She went on to tell my mother that I had musical talent that would find its expression at some point, but it was not piano. In ninth grade, I got my first guitar, and I sat for hours, by myself and with my friends, learning how to play.

I am of the three-chords-and-the-truth camp, and not one of those, like Gregory Abbott, who play and sing fed by the deep musical knowledge that gives them a sense of hopeful abandon. What I do share in common with Abbot and the others is I have to learn my songs by heart to really be able to play them. By definition, improvisors aren't reading music, they are making it, and making it up. They are riffing on what is deep in their bones, and from what they have learned by listening to those around them. Learning chords taught me that they work in relationship. Each key has its own primary color chords, so to speak, and then other chords shade in with nuance, tone, and texture. G, C, and D go together, as do E, A, and B. Whether reading the notes or playing by ear, the only way to learn a song is to practice.

I understand jazz in the same way I understand physics: I know enough to let their metaphors take me to new places. Watching and listening to old school bluegrass players gather around a single mic restates the metaphor in a form that hits closer to home for me, because those folks are playing guitars and singing harmonies I can grasp. The way they position themselves and move in and out to offer their parts is intentional beyond the limitations of the technology. Because they are standing where they can see each other, the harmonizers can watch the lead singer to follow when they end a word or when they breathe so their collective voices rise and fall together. It may not be the open-ended improvisation of a jazz quartet, but it is its own version of one mic, one take.

What all of it boils down to is we have to practice. Practice the chords, practice the transitions, practice listening. Spiritual practice centers around ritual, or meaningful repetition. When the apostle Paul riffs on what love is in 1 Corinthians 13, he plays a song he knew well, and that has become a melody we have been playing along with for centuries:

> Love is patient; love is kind; love is not envious or boastful or arrogant or rude. It does not insist on its own way; it is not irritable or resentful; it does not rejoice in wrongdoing, but rejoices in the truth. It bears all things, believes all things, hopes all things, endures all things. Love never ends.

He keeps going a bit, and then finishes with, "And now faith, hope, and love abide, these three; and the greatest of these is love," describing what it takes to make good music together, if you will.

Good jazz. Good bluegrass. Good harmony. Our practice lives call us to a faith that grows out of listening to one another, a hope that thrives on the uncertainty of improvisation, and a love that incarnates our commitment to inclusion and collaboration.

All of it takes practice.

PRACTICE LISTENING

I AM LOSING MY HEARING for no apparent reason other than, well, my life. Yes, my regular attendance at rock concerts, and the volume of my car radio in my younger years, are responsible for some of the damage, as is standing under a kitchen exhaust fan five or six nights a week for the decade I worked in restaurant kitchens. But there are chefs and musicians my age who don't have to stick mini-transmitters in their ears every morning to be able to hear what is going on. Explaining loss—hearing or otherwise—is not as simple as cause and effect.

I got my first hearing aids about eight years ago. My audiologist at the time told me that most folks finally capitulate to trying them three or four years after they need them. She put the small devices in my ears and told me to walk around the building for a bit to see how they felt. I went down the hallway and returned, amazed at how loud the world was. It reminded me of getting glasses in tenth grade and realizing the lawn was made up of individual blades of grass.

I came back to her office, pulling up and down on my jacket zipper. "Did you know this made noise?"

As I was finishing this book, I got yet another new pair of hearing aids. Ginger and I got home around dusk, and as we walked to the house, I heard a chorus of insects singing. When I commented on the cricket choir, she said, "It's that way every night." I had no idea.

Wearing hearing aids means re-learning how to hear. The ears take in the soundwaves, but the brain does the hearing, delineating the difference between an A-note played on a violin or an electric guitar, or prioritizing a person's voice over the background noise because that's what's most important. When the soundwaves are delivered mechanically, however, the translation process has to be renegotiated. I had to practice giving my brain better directions about what to hear by looking at who was talking, not necessarily because I was trying to lip-read, but because when I faced them and focused on them I could hear better.

Over eight years, the technology of hearing aids has improved, though because most health insurance policies do not cover them, it is expensive to take advantage of the advancements. I wore my first $4000 set for almost four years before we dropped $2500 on a new pair that held promise of improvement. For a year and a half, I went back to the audiologist every month to make adjustments. Each time, I arrived with my observations about the effectiveness of our previous adjustments, and questions about new issues that had come up: The background noise was punishing. I couldn't tell how loud I was talking. I couldn't pick out voices from all that was going on around them. We would make small changes, and I would go try to hear better.

After about a year, my audiologist suggested redoing my hearing tests since things seemed so much worse. I learned that my clarity of hearing—which is not corrected by hearing aids—had diminished 20 percent in my right ear and 40 percent in my left. I was distraught. He sent me to see an ENT doctor because the results were unusual. The doctor scheduled an MRI to see what they could figure out. He was not an alarmist, but said the physical reasons that could cause what was happening could be some sort of blockage, a tumor, or an infection, among other things.

The doctor told me my ears were unremarkable, which I already knew, though what he meant was the test came back clear of all things ominous. I was grateful, but also disappointed that I had no clear answer about the changes in my hearing, other than there was no easy fix. Missing Ginger's side comments—which are funny—struggling to hear in a crowd, and not being able to listen to music easily were my new normal. I had to keep practicing my new way of hearing, even as I was losing sounds that were once within range.

I took my despair to Joan, my spiritual director, who listened and then offered a question in response: "Here's the question for you: how will you listen when you can no longer hear?"

Mark Nepo, an author who lives with hearing loss, says, "We must honor that listening is a personal pilgrimage that takes time and a willingness to circle back." To listen well, we have to circle back to see what we missed, perhaps, or what we failed to take in the first time. To circle back is another way to say practice. To listen to each other, the way musicians do, means paying close attention to what matters in the middle of all the noise that doesn't, and to keep circling back on the verses and choruses until we can hear our part.

The state of my hearing makes me feel as though I am in the extended play version of the story of the blind man who came to Jesus and had to circle back because the first healing didn't do the trick. The man came to Jesus to have his sight restored. Jesus touched him, and the man said, "I can see, but the people look like trees." Jesus touched him again, and the man could see everything.

My audiologist is not quite as efficient as Jesus. I feel like I am continually living the audio version of seeing the trees. He is tenacious, so I keep going back. I keep looking for metaphors to describe what is working and what isn't, and he keeps making adjustments. We are wearing away at it, even as I am discerning what cannot be helped by the hearing aids, as well as different ways to hear and ask for help. I am learning to practice listening, even as my hearing fades.

The root of our word *listen* means to *pay attention to*, a phrase that interests me because it implies that good listening costs us something. We have to pay attention. Who we pay and how much it costs are live questions. We have to let other things go by and focus, drop our presuppositions and be in the moment, lay aside whatever we think we need to say, and listen. We can't sing harmony until we have listened to the melody and paid the attention it takes to respond. We can't take our turn at improvising until we have listened well enough to find our place in the band.

One of the first Bible stories that stuck with me from my childhood was the story of God's call to Samuel. Perhaps it grabbed me because Samuel was a young boy. He lived in the temple with Eli, the priest. Samuel woke in the night because he heard his name. He woke Eli and asked what he wanted, and the old man said he was not the one who had called out. They played the scene a second time, and then a third. The last time, Eli was awake enough to figure out what was going on. "Go back to bed," he said, "and the next time it happens answer, 'Speak, Lord, for your servant is listening.'"

So many of the stories in the Hebrew Bible involve people listening to God and having conversations. Often, God tells them to be quiet and pay attention so they can hear their part. When they become self-absorbed out of pride or despair, God tells them to be quiet and practice listening to sense the connection, to hear their harmony line, and then to have faith—

to trust—that they are not alone. Faith, the writer of the Letter to the Hebrews said, is "the evidence of things hoped for, the substance of things not see." It means trusting that there is more going on than what we can see—or hear.

The word *faith* has long been a challenge for me because it is a noun in English and I think it ought to be a verb, which is amusing because one of my pet peeves is our propensity as Americans to change nouns into verbs. We are a people who value action over being, and our language reflects that. Why do I need to *gift* someone a present when I have always been able to give it to them? We used to *have an impact* and *make a transition*, but now we *impact* others as we *transition* to whatever. But I digress.

I wish faith were a verb because it is an action more than a possession. We most often use *believe* as the substitute verb, but it falls short because believing has more to do with intellectual consent than an act of the will or the heart. Down two thousand years of institutional Christianity, believing has become tied to orthodoxy. Toeing the theological line of correct understanding is not much help when it comes to talking about faith because it is about being true more than about being right. Orthodoxy demands unison. Faith is listening for harmony. It is more about relationship than doctrine; it's not what you believe, but who you trust.

Though many of our church leaders across the centuries were people of deep faith, once the Church as an institution became accustomed to the halls of power, it put the emphasis on "right belief," and perhaps, unwittingly, allowed doctrine to separate belief from relationship. I realize that is a rather audacious summary of Church history, and I think faith is about more than getting our institutional ducks in a row.

We are created in the image of a God who is both steadfast and surprising. We need other verbs, better words. We need language that both grounds and moves us. Belief is a checklist;

faith is a much riskier endeavor. We have to pay attention. We have to listen in order to trust.

Good improvisational musicians are so practiced in the basics that they are ready to not only respond to the unexpected, but to welcome it, in large part because they are intentional listeners. They are paying attention to what those around them are doing, listening for the invitations that come their way, and responding with offerings of their own that grow out of their practice. Improv at its best is not about *it's my turn*, as much as *here's what I can contribute.*

Jesus would have been a great jazz guy because he improvised his life. Most of the encounters with people happened in the context of interruptions. He didn't meet the disciples for breakfast to have them say, "So at nine we need to be at the gate to heal the blind man. Then there's a leper at ten. You have a bit of free time in the desert, until we feed the five thousand at noon. Then we'll scoot across the lake for your afternoon sermon, and then you'll spot Zacchaeus in the tree and go to his house for dinner. Oh, and on the way a woman will touch your cloak because she trusts that you can heal her." Instead, he listened to the day, to his disciples, to those he bumped into, to those who followed or gathered around, and then he responded to what he saw and heard, trusting he had something to offer.

Jazz pianist and composer Oscar Peterson said, "It's the group sound that's important, even when you're playing a solo. You not only have to know your own instrument; you must know the others and how to back them up at all times. That's jazz." That's faith. Life, too. We have to know each other and how to back each other up at all times. I learned how to sing harmony growing up, at Matero Baptist Church in Lusaka, Zambia. All the music was acapella, mostly by necessity. One woman, Rebecca Green, would sing the first line, and then the rest of us would join in, singing and clapping in a variety of complimentary syncopated rhythms. The harmony parts were not written. We listened and then offered what we found.

As I go through the course of my week, I hear what appears to be a whole lot of solo performances: the person who makes my salad at the Marketplace; Ginger sitting next to me at a coffee shop as we work on separate projects; my brother calling to catch up on life; the woman at the Dunkin' Donuts on Madison Avenue, who somehow manages to remember my order, even though she only sees me on Mondays. If I think of their actions toward me as starting points, like Rebecca singing the first line, I hear Peterson's admonition to back them up at all times in a new way. How can I best back them up? How do I honor their moment? How do I listen to their lives? I'm not speaking of some sort of grand gesture, but my offering in the moments we share. Am I attentive? Am I present? Do they know I am listening?

Jesus leaned hard on the privileged people of his day to pay attention to the poor. When a woman broke the alabaster jar and poured expensive perfume on Jesus' feet, the privileged ones around him went ballistic. Did he have any idea how much money was wasted? He just smiled and asked if they could hear the melody of her heart well enough to back her up.

The melody of faith is an ancient song that has to be learned by heart, which is my favorite way of saying you have to practice until you can play and sing in a way that it bubbles out of you. Our present and our future are tethered to the great cloud of witnesses who have already played their songs and have left a myriad of melodies for us to listen to and learn. When we pass the bread and cup at communion, we do so with all of those who have come before us. Just as we back one another up in this life, we must also keep reminding ourselves that the band has been playing for far longer than our part of the song. To remember is to also embrace the grief over what and who has been lost. Those days are gone. Those people are gone. We are here. Together. For now.

The gospel writers set down their stories so we could listen and join in, which means doing more than merely repeating what was handed down. We listen and then offer our versions, remembering the stories with the voices and instruments we have.

Nora Gallagher says faith "is not about belief in something irrational or about a blind connection to something unreal. It's about a gathering, an accumulation of events and experiences of a different order." The first time I read that sentence, I thought she said faith was about putting events in a different order. "I love that," I jotted in the margins. "Remember and reorder."

My misreading reminded me that our lives are a litany of losses, even as they are a contagion of grace and gratitude. In any given moment, we cannot see what is coming next, which means we have to keep remembering and reordering as the context around us changes.

And things have changed. I haven't ridden the train to Manhattan in months because of COVID-19. I wonder how my coffee people and the bagel guy in the small cart at Madison and East 35th have survived the days of no pedestrians. Closer to home, I have spent weeks sitting at our dining room table rather than my window seat at the Marketplace. I am riding a metaphor of improvisational jazz in a time when all the clubs are closed and we are living our lives at a distance from one another. If improv takes practice, how do we rehearse for a scene we never expected?

What Gallagher actually said was faith connects us to "experiences of a different order," which is another way of saying that faith is not about digging in—as in, *God said it, I believe it, that settles it.* If life were ten minutes long, that might be a viable stance, but life is long and difficult and serendipitous, and Jesus said, "Follow me," without offering many specifics. We are called to reorder our understanding, our perspective, and our relationships because of what and how we choose to remember the story of God in our lives, even as there is still more light to break forth.

There are fresh new lines of faith to trace. Our lives are a succession of before's and after's. Life before my parents died was not the same as the life I know now. Nor is life the same as before we moved to Guilford, or before I began my job as an editor, or before I got up this morning. In order for God to grow up with me, and me with God, I have to remember and reorder my life the way I have had to reorder how I move and cook in my kitchen every time we change houses, along with remembering the recipes.

To tell the story—to remember—is to take our place in it as well, even as it changes our lives, which means we have to practice trust. The melody of faith is the tune of trust, of dependence, of vulnerability, of keeping promises, of leaning on the everlasting arms. It is not the music of blind allegiance, unquestioning adherence, or orthodoxy. Faith is not just going along because that is what we are supposed to do. It is trusting when we do not completely understand, or when we are not able to see the whole picture. The substance of things not seen.

One of the blessings of my life is that I was able to live near the ocean for a time. For seven years, we lived in the Green Harbor neighborhood of Marshfield, Massachusetts. Our house was six hundred fifty feet from Cape Cod Bay. Our beach was the edge of America. To look out over the vast expanse of water was both humbling and encouraging. The ebb and flow of the tides was a new way to tell time for me, though the rhythm of the waves is as old as creation, a song that invited me to chime in with appropriate insignificance.

To think of those days, watching the Schnauzers run down the beach, makes me think of one of those childhood songs I have sung more times than I can count: "I've got love like an ocean in my soul." That is the third verse, actually. It starts with "Peace like a river," and then "Joy like a fountain." But when it gets to the verse about faith, it strays from the water—at least in the version I learned: "I've got faith like an anchor."

Though I understand the imagery, it misses the mark. The point of an anchor is to hold you safe in the harbor, to keep you in place, not send you sailing down the river or across the sea. If love is an ocean, joy is a fountain, peace is a river, or life is a storm, faith cannot be about hunkering down or playing it safe.

If the metaphor is about what we do on the water, then the line needs to be, "I've got faith like a rowboat." If love is an ocean, then faith is what keeps us afloat. To go out on the water means we must trust what we can't control. The ocean that is God's love calls us out of the harbor, into the open sea, and out beyond our comfort zones. We set out in the frailest of vessels, trusting that we will not ever reach a place where we will run out of love's reach. Faith is trusting that love will not let us go, that there's a wideness in God's mercy, like the wideness of the sea, that the deep, deep love of Jesus is underneath and around us. Whatever these days may hold, whatever might have been, whatever has yet to happen, we have love like an ocean, deeper and wider than any circumstance or loneliness, and that is what will keep me afloat in our little row boats of faith.

In the months that followed each of my parent's deaths, the heaviest hour of the week for me was Sunday morning worship. I have never completely grasped why, except to say in that the thin place, grief hit me hardest, and the service music was a big part in both the weight and the comfort I experienced. Maybe that is why the anchor does not work for me. I am not looking to sink, or to get weighed down. I don't want to be anchored. I want to know what will keep us afloat. This is not a period of safe harbor in my life. I am not looking to stay put. I am at sea, far away from much of what I have known for sure, following those who have charted this course ahead of me, listening as hard as I can, and wondering what will happen next. In the midst of it all,

I can say we have peace like a river, and love like an ocean, and I want faith like a rowboat.

The problem with my metaphor is the rowboat conjures up a picture of a solitary person in a little boat out on the sea. Yet again, I come back to my mantra: faith is a team sport, a group effort—just like jazz. None of us are alone on the ocean, or navigating the rapids, or even floating down a lazy river on a sunny afternoon. We need a bigger boat—a wider image—which is why, I suppose, I keep mixing metaphors. After all, we know, down to the basic particles of our existence, that we can't keep going by ourselves. Our energies feed off of one another. All of creation is connected.

We need only to listen, trust, pray.

PRACTICE IMPROVISING

YEARS AGO, SCOTT PECK WROTE A BOOK called *The Road Less Traveled*, which began, "Life is difficult." He was not saying something new. He was restating the obvious, even as he was saying something important, something true that is still worth repeating. When we face difficulty in our lives—tragedy, grief, sorrow, hardship—we are not facing something other than life. Life is difficult because it is life. Life is also uncertain, which brings me back to the jazz band, sitting close, practiced in the art of the unexpected familiarity of improvisation. They are listening, playing the basic form, and then one stands up to improvise, which is a risky move. They have prepared, but who knows what will happen next. They are playing songs of hope.

The root meaning of improvisation is *internally preparing*, or getting ready for what you can't see. In John Irving's *A Prayer for Owen Meany*, Owen practices a basketball shot over the course of his life, with the help of his friend John, because he believes he is God's instrument. He is convinced his preparation matters, even though he cannot see why. Even though his life was full of challenges and tragedy, he practiced hope.

Hope is richer than optimism, more complex than the determinism of cause and effect. Hope knows that life is not a romantic comedy that will formulaically resolve itself as the credits roll. Hope knows that doing the right thing will not automatically cause good things to happen. Hope knows life is not fair, and hope knows things will change; in the uncertainty that comes with change is the possibility that life will not stay the way it is. Hope keeps improvising to see what else the song will bring.

The closing line to Stephen King's novella, *Rita Hayworth and the Shawshank Redemption*, finds the narrator, Ellis "Red" Redding, violating his parole and riding a bus from Maine to Texas, following the promises of his friend Andy, who escaped to Mexico.

> I find I am excited, so excited I can hardly hold the pencil in my trembling hand. I think it is the excitement that only a free man can feel, a free man starting a journey whose conclusion is not certain.
>
> I hope Andy is down there.
>
> I hope I can make it across the border.
>
> I hope to see my friend and shake his hand.
>
> I hope the Pacific is as blue as it has been in my dreams.
>
> I hope.

Hoping is not wishing. Hoping is not believing. Hope put Mary and Joseph on the road, sent the shepherds running into town without regard for the sheep, and made John the Baptist call out the proud and powerful. Rebecca Solnit says, "Hope is not a door, but a sense that there might be a door at some point, some way out of the problems of the present moment even before that way is found or followed."

Behind our house is an old barn that we have worked hard to fix up. Before we moved into the house, the church had used the barn as storage space. It was packed to the roof with things intended for the church fair, with things no one knew what to do with but didn't want to throw away, and with things that just somehow ended up there. I even found the base to what had been one of the columns on the front of the church. Along with the stuff, we found evidence of a number of various creatures who had taken up residence in the building. After folks from the church cleared the place out, we worked hard for a couple weeks to clean and repair, and then to paint and furnish the old building.

It has become a room rich with memories, even in our short time here. We have regular barn dinners with a wonderful mixture of folks. Since it has no heat, it is a mostly three-season venue, though we do host Cookies and Carols the last Sunday of Advent. This year, it has sat silent because of the pandemic.

Our first spring, as we were setting up for Beer and Hymns, Ginger called me over to see the sparrow's nest she had found on an empty bookshelf, tucked into an old Red Sox hat. There were eggs in it. Instead of worrying about who was going to find her nest outside, one sparrow tucked her nest away on an empty shelf in our mostly empty barn. It must have felt safer than outdoors. Little did she know that we could have swept it all away in one motion.

Safety does not last long for sparrows, or for us.

I looked at that little nest—so much effort put into creating a place where her eggs could hatch, and for her new little ones to grow to build nests of their own—and I heard Jesus' words of seeming comfort:

> Are not two sparrows sold for a penny? Yet not
> one of them will fall to the ground apart from
> God....So do not be afraid; you are of more value
> than many sparrows.

The reason Jesus used sparrows to make his point is they were birds of little value on most any scale. They were not regarded as useful or pretty. They were just little birds. If something happened to one of them, nobody really noticed. Except God. Jesus' metaphor is about something other than a happy ending. He never says anything about God catching the falling sparrows. He says God knows when they fall. So do not be afraid.

The admonition not to fear is one of the most repeated phrases in scripture. The angel says it to Mary when he comes with news that she will have a son, and also to Joseph when he gets the word that his fiancée is going to have a baby that he knew nothing about. In Genesis, an angel says it to Hagar, an enslaved woman who was owned by Abraham and Sarah, as much as Sarah could own anything, being property herself. Some versions translate the word as servant or concubine, but the reality was Hagar had no choices of her own in her life. She was forced to have a son with Abraham because Sarah thought she couldn't have children, and the custom of the day said Hagar's son would be Abraham's legal heir. Then Sarah got pregnant and became jealous of Hagar and her son, Ishmael. She told Abraham to banish them to the desert—to send them out to die. They wandered around, finding nothing to eat or drink, until finally Hagar left her son to die under a bush and walked away, trying to get out of earshot of the boy's crying, when an angel found them and said, "What troubles you, Hagar? Do not be afraid; for God has heard the voice of the boy where he is."

The angel's question is an oddly humorous moment in the story. Hagar had come to the place where she had abandoned her son because she couldn't watch his suffering, and the angel showed up and said, "What troubles you, Hagar?"

I picture her turning around and saying, "Are you kidding me? What troubles me?"

The angel was undaunted. "Do not be afraid; for God has heard the voice of the boy where he is." You can't bear to hear it anymore, but God hears the boy. Do not be afraid—in your difficulty, in your pain, in your despair. The story is not over yet.

At the beginning of the First World War, Virginia Woolf, who had her own struggle with depression, wrote in her journal, "The future is dark, which is on the whole, the best thing the future can be, I think."

Nighttime is its own incarnate metaphor. We have used it to name what is unknown, scary, disorienting, or depressing. Light has been the symbol of insight and discovery, of hope and possibility. Here is another place where I am learning about both the power and the limitations of metaphor.

Our words and images often carry more than one meaning. The conventional contrast between day and night, or light and darkness, takes on new layers—or at least, new for me—as I listen to people of color describe what they hear in those words, or what it feels like to be the *dark* ones when the images used to convey clarity or cleanliness are white. In the same way that I, as a male, had to listen and learn from women that *man* and *mankind* do not include all people any more than *he* as a pronoun can stand for a female. I am learning to examine my vocabulary around light and dark, and black and white, and learning—again—to remember that what I intend in my metaphor is not always the same as the impact of my words. It requires more of me than saying there are shadows in the daylight and stars at night. As Oscar Peterson said, it's the group that's important—and I'm not the leader of the band.

When I go to New York City, I ride the train and then walk about ten minutes from Grand Central Station to my office. I expect the sidewalks to be crowded with people moving with apparent focus and determination. We all watch the crossing lights and the cars, and pay little attention to one another, other than to avoid collisions.

In the crush of people trying to get through the doors at Grand Central one afternoon, I saw an elderly woman with a walker a few yards in front of me. A young man got to the door ahead of her but didn't see her at first. He was doing what he did every afternoon. Just as I was about to speed up to see if I could get the door, I saw her presence register in his peripheral vision, and even though he had already gone through the door, he improvised and turned back to hold it open. Then he smiled as he waited for her to get through. It was a small gesture for everyone except the woman.

Hope is not believing that everything will get better, as much as it is trusting that we are here for each other. Hope is living as though it matters that we notice the details, that every note we play has some significance. Hope is holding open the door, even when we're in a hurry—trusting that our actions may not feel indelible, but they are remembered. Significance is often more a matter of impact than intent.

For over twenty years of my life I have lived in New England, which means I have become accustomed to the gray and cold of winter. Even more, I have come to love the spirit that rises up in people when we have a winter storm. However heavy the snow might fall, as soon as we can we are digging out and getting on with our lives. It doesn't matter how high the parking lot mountains get, we shovel our walks, clean off our cars, dress in layers, and keep on living. But the weather takes its toll. We use the verb *weathered* to mean worn down. Leave something outside long enough and it will give way to the weather. Even a sparrow knows that. "History is like weather," Solnit says. "Weather doesn't stop. That's why you can't save anything."

As someone who grew up Baptist, there's something deep inside me that hears the word *saved* and remembers all that I was told Jesus saved me from—most notably death and myself. Being saved meant I was "in the world but not of it." I was taught that what mattered most was something other than this life. I was saved for heaven and saved from here. Whatever this life was, it was not my primary concern. My hope was not of this world, as if the underlying prayer is, "Dear God, please tell me this is temporary."

The paradox of the Incarnation is that life is temporary and significant. God is with us, in us, as one of us. Jesus' words and actions are more visceral than the promise of a heaven to be named later. Jesus said the realm of God is ikn us, among us, within us. However we translate the preposition, what matters is right here, right now. Yes, he told his disciples of mansions to come, but he spent more time talking to them about forgiving one another, about living out love in practical and uncomfortable ways, and about speaking truth to power. Jesus never encouraged anyone to lose hope in the present moment. He knew life was messy and hard and as relentless and unpredictable as the weather, that the hopes and fears of all the years showed up on a daily basis, and that sparrows were dropping. He talked about the hope in the poor and the meek and the mourning who were digging out of their lives and going on together. And he knew the only way to live was to spend it all—spend the grief and the grace, spend the sadness and the heartache, spend the compassion and the camaraderie. "Take up your cross," he said. Don't save a thing.

John Berger says hope is "the action of approach, of measuring distances and walking towards." The word approach makes me think of walking up to the altar for communion, standing in the unbroken line of saints who have come before us, who point us to the horizon even as we feel the push of those who will come after us, expecting the path of discipleship to remain worn—weathered. I also think of communion as we pass the plates down the pews, offering and receiving, approaching one another in the name of Christ, reaching out as we give and take. Approach: the peace of Christ be with you; and also with you.

Measuring distances. "Teach us to measure our days," is another way to read Psalm 90. And so we mark forty days from Ash Wednesday to Easter, not counting Sundays, even as we also count the days of Advent, Christmastide, Eastertide. And Ordinary Time. God has shown us how far it is to forgiveness, how close by grace resides, how long and wide and deep and tall the love of Christ truly is.

Walking towards. One of the choruses we sing with some regularity at church is, "We are walking in the light of God." Jesus knew he had come from God and was going to God; we follow in his steps. We walk towards God, towards love, towards justice, towards kindness, towards uncertainty, towards hope, towards making sure everyone knows they are wonderfully created in the image of God, and worthy to be loved.

I saw comedian Wayne Brady, who is a master of improvisation, perform many years ago. The show began with one of his staff coming out with a flip chart and a magic marker. He asked for forty words from the audience. As we shouted things out, he wrote them down, one to a page: summer, penguin, casserole, underpants....You get the idea. When he was finished, the drummer began playing a hip hop rhythm, and Brady came on stage and began to freestyle as his staff member flipped the pages, revealing the words we had written, one by one. Brady's rhymes never missed a beat. He had never seen the words before, but he had prepared. He knew how to trust himself, to step into the moment, to give it everything he had, and to make us feel a part of what he was doing. He made it look easy. It was not. I wondered how many times he failed before he could get through all the words as he practiced.

Leaning into uncertainty means we will be well acquainted with failure. The word makes us flinch because too often we equate failure with losing, as in not winning. They are not the same thing. Losing implies a competition. Life, at its core, is not that, despite our American obsession with being number one. The narrative of scripture is one of both failure and loss, in the sense of grief. When I plant seeds in my garden, part of the reality is that some will fail to grow. The sperm that fertilizes an egg in the womb is one among millions, even billions, of failures. I think failure, like the weather, is inevitable.

Failure can mean more than one thing. We can talk about failure of outcomes and also failure of process. In the tech world, people are encouraged to fail faster. It is not hard to find stories of those who set out to invent one thing, only to find something unexpected in their failure. We also talk about being a failure. You don't have to read far into my writing to find these words: you are wonderfully and uniquely created in the image of God, and worthy to be loved. Failure, as a noun, does not apply to people. We fail; we are not failures.

I do not intend to romanticize failure. It hurts. It damages. It has consequences. Some years ago, I was speaking at a college and I thought I was offering an encouraging word when I said that I thought failure was one of God's organizing principles, meaning that God can work in any circumstance. Afterwards, one of the students came up to talk, saddened by the reality that his grades were not good enough to get into medical school, which was his dream. It was not going to happen. He was a senior in college, and he was not sure what to do. He was faced with his future not being what he had hoped. My improvisation on failure had not been helpful.

I didn't have an answer for him. There wasn't an answer. Now, seven years later, I wonder what happened to him. He was bright and faithful and grieving. I wonder what he found beyond failure, or because of it.

Frederick Buechner has a sermon on the Crucifixion titled, "The Magnificent Defeat," meaning that to get to the hope of the Resurrection, we must live with the reality of the cataclysmic failure of Jesus' death. The accounts of the disciples after the Crucifixion show that they were left lost and wandering by Jesus' execution. They hid. They walked home. They went fishing. None of them waxed eloquent about Jesus' death being a moral victory, or praised the power of the atonement. It felt like the one on whom they had staked their lives had failed.

Did Jesus fail? The answer begs another question: What was Jesus trying to do? And another: Was the morning after his death the best time to evaluate his life?

I got the job that best fits my skills the summer before I turned sixty. I have done lots of things for money. I have never been the one who planned to hang around for the gold watch. Some of my job changes were born out of failure. I applied to do doctoral work in Switzerland, but my letter got lost on the desk of the professor I contacted because he had a heart attack. I entered a clinical pastoral education program (CPE) as a way of making meaning in the meantime. In other words, I became a hospital chaplain because I failed to get into the PhD program. When the professor recuperated enough to write back, I had found a new place to be. I stayed at the hospital for four years and never made it to Switzerland.

I became a substitute teacher, and Ginger managed a group home for struggling adolescents because we needed salaries as we tried to plant a church in Charlestown, a downtown neighborhood in Boston. Our church-planting efforts were a spectacular failure. My days as the building sub at Charlestown High School turned into a position as an English teacher. I became a chef because the kitchen was a depression-free zone for me, but also because I failed to be able to continue teaching.

That description of my employment history is one way to tell the story. I can also tell it from the perspective of my sense of calling and vocation, and how those who have loved and supported me helped me improvise and find my way. The two tellings are not mutually exclusive.

Our middle Schnauzer, Lila, is wonderful at failing. She gets excited when she sees us, and jumps without measuring the distance, which means she often falls short. She gets up, shakes her head, and jumps again, trusting she can get to us. She's a failer—not a failure.

I learned that word years ago from the title of Kathleen Edwards's debut record. *Failer*, as in one who fails. Maybe that's a better word than sinner. Failers are saved by grace, and by grace, learn to keep jumping and trusting that love will catch us, even when we don't know what's coming next.

Failure is the key to, but not the last word in, improvisation. One of the main tenets of improv theater is, *Say yes*. Whatever the situation, go all in. Give it a shot. You are not alone. Even when everything works, there are things worth revising. It is interesting to me that I can find recordings of improvisational jazz, which means, oxymoronically, that there is a way the song should go. Going back to Gregory Abbott's "(one mic, one take)," if I am trying to learn the song from the video, I am going to take his once-in-a-lifetime version as the way the song is supposed to go.

We do the same thing with scripture when we say, "The Bible says...," as though the words mean the same thing every time, regardless of context. If we allow ourselves to buy into the idea that God's will is a plan we either succeed or fail to follow, we will miss the shades of grace and hope in our lives.

We are not following a set of directives, but the call of relationship, which is rife with both failure and forgiveness.

PRACTICE BELONGING

FIGURING OUT WHERE OUR WORDS came from sometimes produces interesting images, like *metaphor* coming from the Greek word for porter. Some of the words with Germanic or Anglo-Saxon roots are less poetic. *Belong* is one of those. *Be-* is a variant of *by*, as in *next to*; *long* is, well, long, as in a long time. *Belong*: be next to one another for a long time. You can hear it in the wedding vows where couples promise to stay until they die. In families that find ways to stay connected over years and wounds and circumstances. Walk into most any church, and they will say that you are welcome. The ones worth going back to are the ones committed to the practice of belonging.

My friend Terry, repeating the words of another friend, says love is "shared loss," which is another way of saying love does what it needs to do to stand by for a long time, especially when things get tough.

Ben E. King was on to something when he sang that all he wanted was for someone to stand by him. Belong. When we use the word, we talk about it as something we feel or want, but it requires others to make room for it to happen. I can't stand by anyone unless they stand there, too.

Howard Thurman wrote, "The will to understand other people is a most important part of the personal equipment of those who would share in the unfolding idea of human fellowship." When I read the word *fellowship*, it makes me think of sailing together. Belonging.

Thurman's words also remind me of a story I heard from a pastor in Durham, North Carolina, an African-American man who worked in a part of town that has not experienced much benefit from the city's recent economic resurgence. A group from a predominantly white church in town came to spend a week helping in the neighborhood, which is made up predominantly of people of color. The folks from the church wanted to make a difference. They meant well. They wore t-shirts with the name of their church on the front. On the back were Jesus' words from Matthew 25:40: "Truly I tell you, just as you did it to one of the least of these who are members of my family, you did it to me." They didn't have the will to understand, to share the loss. They didn't come to the neighborhood to belong. Belonging requires more than meaning well. It is the practice of together-ness.

When Ginger and I officiate weddings, we often say that the promises made in the ceremony have to be kept every day. That's how you keep a lifelong promise: over and over and over. We have to keep the promises we make to each other and to God, on a daily basis, and reinterpret what it means to keep them as we learn more about each other. Meaning well is not enough. Love is an act of will. To love is to practice belonging.

Sam Wells, an Anglican priest and writer, says the most important word in the Bible is *with*, which is another way of saying *stand by*. The image makes me think of the old story about the man who fell into a hole that was deeper than he was tall. The sides were slick, and he could not figure out how to get out, so he began to call for help. Many people passed by without stopping. Some stopped but did not offer meaningful assistance. Finally, one man stopped and stayed at the opening of the hole.

"Please," the man implored, "help me."

The other man jumped down into the hole.

"Great, now we're both down here."

"Yes," said the second man, "but I've been down here before."

The angel looked at Joseph, Jesus' father whose world was crumbling around him, and said, "Name the child Emmanuel— God with us." (Though I'm quite sure the angel didn't translate the name into English.)

If we do not practice belonging, we will not have a song to play. In the fall of 1986, I was in Manhattan with my friend Billy for just a day or two. Neither of us knew our way around the city, other than we knew to go to Greenwich Village to hear music. Thanks to a flyer stapled to a telephone pole, we happened upon Toots Thielemans, Stanley Clarke, and McCoy Tyner sitting in together in a small club below street level. Billy is a musician. He recognized the names. On my own, I would never have known what I could have missed. Any one of the men could have filled the room for a solo gig. They didn't need each other to draw a crowd. Instead, they chose to be together. They needed each other to make the music they wanted to make.

I knew hardly any of the songs they played, but I was mesmerized. Like any good jazz trio, they took turns playing lead and backup. You could see how they trusted each other, as well as themselves, in the way they played together.

Billy and I knew no one else in the room that night, yet because of how those three played together, we walked out into the New York night feeling like we belonged.

LEAVING A MARK

LIFE SENTENCE

In the grammar of grace,
love runs through sentence after sentence,
punctuated by periods of pain,
ellipses of hope, commas of community,
spaces of serenity, and fundaments of forgiveness,
while the syntax of the cynic depends on
dangling doubt off fragments of fear, phrases fraught
with the alliteration of alienation,
and interjections of judgment.
There is little benefit in being bilingual.

PUNCTUATION IS NO SMALL THING. The difference between "Let's eat, Grandma" and "Let's eat Grandma" is the difference between a family dinner and a Donner Party Thanksgiving. The same is true for stories from scripture. In John's gospel, Jesus and his disciples encounter a man who was born blind. Here is how the encounter has been most often translated and punctuated:

> His disciples asked him, "Rabbi, who sinned, this
> man or his parents, that he was born blind?" Jesus
> answered, "Neither this man nor his parents
> sinned; he was born blind so that God's works
> might be revealed in him. We must work the
> works of him who sent me while it is day; night is
> coming when no one can work. As long as I am in
> the world, I am the light of the world."

The disciples wanted to know who was to blame for the blindness. Their question carried a tone of judgment, whether or not they looked down on the man. Their theological frame assumed that the man's disability had to be someone's fault; that is how they had been taught to make sense of tragedy. Someone sinned, and the man was left to live with the consequences. The only question was who was to blame. The translators appear to share that perspective because their punctuation has led to Jesus' answer often being taken to mean that God made the man blind so he could heal him: "...he was born blind so that God's works might be revealed in him," as though God was setting the stage for a miracle, or somehow made it happen.

That's not a theological perspective I can live with. I don't think God makes things happen to show off, or dishes out difficulty as punishment. My friend Kenny suggests that we re-punctuate the passage, to let the grace shine through.

> Jesus answered, "Neither this man nor his parents
> sinned. He was born blind. So that God's works
> might be revealed in him, we must work the
> works of the One who sent me while it is day;
> night is coming when no one can work. As long
> as I am in the world, I am the light of the world."

He was born blind. *Period.* So God can shine through, we must be the conduits of insight and healing.

The punctuation matters. In the second telling, Jesus reframes the disciples' question and calls them to see the man's plight as a story of pain rather than one of guilt. Guilt calls for judgement; pain offers an invitation for compassion and connection. For grace and healing. There is a difference between being broken and being damned. God does not purposely punctuate our lives with blame.

Literary critic Stanley Fish says a writer is "someone who loves sentences." It's not just about loving words, but how they team up to make meaning. Joe Moran says, "Skilled writers write in sentences not because sentences are what we write (although they are), but because they write small." Punctuation helps a group of words become a sentence.

The sentences that make up the stories of our lives require a variety of punctuation marks. I learned to write in a primary school in Lusaka, Zambia, with British teachers who called a period a "full stop." The name describes what the small dot was designed to do. A full stop is an ending. Period. We can't just roll through as though it were a suggestion.

As we grow older, life's sentences have more periods, more endings, which means we have to start new sentences to see what comes after those endings for as long as we have a story to tell. I don't think it is as simple as saying every ending has a new beginning, yet there are befores and afters. Endings are part of the deal.

One afternoon, before a Christmas that is now a distant memory, I was in the self-checkout line at a Kroger in Durham when the guy in front of me started talking. He was in his early twenties, a good four inches taller than me, and in a Kroger uniform. He had a single Christmas card in his hand. He began talking about how the management didn't get why they needed more checkout stations, and how they wanted to expand produce when the guy who has worked in produce for thirty-five years knew it was a big mistake. His stream-of-consciousness rant about the perils in produce and the catastrophe at checkout continued until, without the slightest punctuation, he said, "And my dad died last March eleventh and I'm the one who found him and Christmas used to be a really big deal to my family and I didn't want to work today and now we're all getting together and we don't really know what to do." The unexpected period on his run-on grief came when they called him to step up to the empty terminal and checkout. He paid for his card, looked back at me, said, "Merry Christmas," and walked away.

In the past, I have used the metaphor of a run-on sentence to describe life. Now I'm not so sure. Those convicted of heinous crimes are given a life sentence, which takes the story out of it. The endless run-on of incarceration is not redemptive because there is nowhere to go. A sentence that doesn't end is dehumanizing. We all need a story to make sense of the sentences. We need some sort of punctuation to help us see how to separate the words and phrases that help us tell the story.

In my work as an editor, I keep relearning the importance and power of revision. Time, distance, and eyes other than the author's help turn a draft into a story. Alongside colors and music stands the metaphor of reworking the punctuation of our lives to tell our stories in a new way. *Revise*, at its root, means to see again. Then we rewrite: we inscribe it again.

The sentences of our lives are not handed down like prison terms, but can be crafted the way a writer rewrites for clarity and meaning. *Repentance* is the stained-glass synonym for revision: a turning, a retelling of the story, a re-punctuating of the sentence to say it a different way, to emphasize, or to clarify. *Reconcile* means to gather again in a new way. *Repeat* comes from words that mean to look for again. *Remember* means to put things back together, whether a puzzle or a memory. Even a story that feels finished to us can be revised and retold.

Sentences are more than beginnings and endings. So are our lives. We have things that give us pause, that take us aback, that deserve greater attention, that require more time. We have marks to leave for all of those things.

COMMAS OF CARE

THE NOVEL *A TO X: A STORY IN LETTERS*, has only two characters. A'ida writes to her husband Xavier, who is a political prisoner. The whole story is told in her letters found in his cell after his death. We never hear from him. In one letter she says:

> When I buy baklava, which is not often because I eat too many, I leave a few for her on her windowsill, with a head scarf over them so the wasps don't come. For these little gifts we don't thank each other with words. They are commas of care.... Commas of care! Punctuating our days with them is something long-term prisoners learn, isn't it?

Commas of care: compassion by punctuation.

For many years, my denomination, the United Church of Christ, quoted Gracie Allen—"Never put a period where God has placed a comma"—as a part of their *God Is Still Speaking* campaign. One of the ways the comma is defined is as a *soft pause* in a sentence. It is not a full stop, but a rest or a small break.

I found this advice in one guide: "The presence or absence of a comma can change the meaning of a sentence—sometimes dramatically." Perhaps even more so with commas of care. The soft pauses in the sentences of our life stories offer us the chance to show kindness and compassion. In the endless stream of raging rhetoric that passes for conversation in our culture, the moments that offer us pause are life-giving. We are called to punctuate our days with care, to offer glimpses of our shared humanity and remind one another of our unbreakable belonging.

Packing up our house in Durham to move to Guilford felt like an archaeological expedition through the layers of our life, not only because of the collections of things that had to be sorted and assigned a destination, but also because of the memories we unearthed. One that came to the surface was a favorite from my days as the youth minister at University Baptist Church in Fort Worth, Texas:

One Wednesday evening, I was walking down the hall of the building, getting ready for the night's activities, when I passed Hazel, one of the young people, coming the other way.

For no particular reason other than to greet her, I said, "Hey—I like you, and I tell people that even when you're not around."

We smiled at each other and kept going in our set directions.

A couple days later, I received a card from her in which she told me she'd had an awful day at school, and my passing comment had reminded her she was loved.

"You made my day," she said.

I can remember sitting at my desk with the card and thinking I needed to mark the moment. What felt like incidental contact was a comma of care. I had re-punctuated her day. I meant what I said to Hazel, but I wasn't aiming for a life-changing encounter.

The things we set in motion with our words and actions, however small they might seem, take on a life of their own.

Later on in our packing, Ginger found a letter my father had written to me in August 2006, when we still lived in Marshfield and my depression was at its heaviest. I had started writing about it in my blog the previous December. The public nature of my disclosure was new for me and for my family.

My dad was not one who spoke about his feelings. When he needed to get to something, he wrote it down. His letter was full of compassion and empathy. He was working hard to connect with me, telling me about times in his own life when he had struggled with depression. He also told me that his best friend battled depression most of his life. Most of what he revealed was new information for me. In the last paragraphs, he wrote:

> What I pray you will get from this letter is the understanding that you are loved, accepted, and prayed for. To express to you how proud I am of you would be impossible. You are the most multi-gifted person I have ever known. My heart overflows with memories of joy and excitement in watching you grow and develop.
>
> In reading some of your blogs it seems that I am the source of some of your heartache. If so, I am saying to you I am very sorry. I can say in all honesty that not in any way did I intend to create problems for you. You are the pride and joy of my life—I love you.
>
> Sincerely,
>
> Dad

As I continue to note, my father is dead, but my story with him is not over. I am still turning periods into commas, and sometimes, vice versa. I am still remembering our life together and revising how I think of him and of us as new insights arise.

Rereading the letter made me think about Hazel walking down the hall because I realized that some of my incidental contact with my father over the years had left him with the impression that my struggles were his fault, which had not been my intention any more than I had intended to do offer Hazel a friendly greeting.

I am grateful to be able to look back and say that in the time between my father's letter and his death, I had the chance to let him know he wasn't responsible for my depression. We both got better at forgiving one another. When I think about Dad's letter and Hazel in the hallway, I pray that my kindness is more than random, that my commas of care are intentional punctuation. Incidental contact can be on purpose, even in a passing moment. It's worth remembering that in the more consistent relationships in our lives, the layers of incidental contact stack up into patterns and rituals that either build pathways to our hearts or walls around them.

Until my mother died, she and I shared a Thanksgiving tradition, even though we were rarely together on Thanksgiving after I graduated from seminary. I called during my first Thanksgiving away from her and asked for her cornbread dressing recipe. She shared it and then said, "Don't write it down. I want you to call every Thanksgiving and ask for it." That is what I did, even though I had the recipe memorized.

She died in January 2016. The night before Thanksgiving, I told Ginger that I had no one to call for the recipe. I also mentioned it to my brother and sister-in-law, whom Ginger had arranged to surprise me for the holiday.

About ten o'clock Thanksgiving morning, my phone rang. It was Marissa, our niece-in-law.

"Uncle Milton," she said, "I'm calling to ask for your mom's dressing recipe." In a sentence, she turned a full stop into a comma of care. I read her the recipe and then gave her the same instructions my mother gave to me. Marissa has called every Thanksgiving since.

After I hung up, I found out my brother had been the editor of our sentence and had changed the period to a comma. He had prompted Marissa to call me. I remain grateful for our story together and all there is yet to tell.

My father's stepmother lived with depression. She was who I knew as Grandma C because his birth mother died a month after he was born. I was working as a chaplain at Baylor Medical Center in Dallas, when Grandma C was hospitalized because the depression was so severe. She was there for several weeks. As things got better, she began to think about what she could do to help herself. She felt the suffocating self-focus of the illness and decided to respond by writing letters. She went through her address book and wrote everyone in it over the course of a few weeks. She was honest about her depression, and she told people she needed to hear from them.

By the time of her hospitalization, she had been a widow for almost forty years. One of the people she wrote was a man, Roy, whom she and her husband had known in Arizona when they were newlyweds. Roy was married at the time. His wife died around the time my grandfather did. Roy remarried. He answered my grandmother's letter to tell her his second wife had died about a year earlier. They began a correspondence that became a relationship. When they were both eighty, they decided to get married. I had the honor of officiating their wedding. They were married for seventeen years before he died.

As I began to learn how to live with depression, I found hope in her story, not because it was a happy ending, as much as I had seen her change the punctuation of her life.

A'ida told her incarcerated husband that "long-term prisoners" were the ones who knew how to punctuate with commas of care. Though prison would not necessarily be my working metaphor for life, after the early months of the pandemic, we all understand more about what it means to feel sequestered by circumstance, and even choice. In the days since, we have watched people we love die, seen places we love close, and become more familiar than we would like with endings. Changing our periods to commas of care is a gift we can give one another and ourselves.

A pause, a breath, a rest. A sense that the thought is not yet complete, the moment is not yet over.

Lord, teach us to punctuate our days.

SEMI-COLONS OF CONTINUATION

ONE OF THE SURPRISES OF GRIEF for me was that marking the second anniversary of the deaths of my parents was more difficult than the first. My father died on August 3, 2013. In the difficult second summer, the solstice was not lost on me. I could feel the days begin to get shorter and heavier, even in late July. I read an article about Project Semicolon, an organization founded by a woman named Amy Bluell, who struggled with depression for many years. She became so despairing that she attempted suicide. The explanation for the name of the organization read, "A semicolon is used when an author could've chosen to end their sentence but chose not to. The author is you, and the sentence is your life."

As one who lives with depression, I was moved by the community they were working to cultivate. As one in the throes of grief, I was strengthened by the invitation to solidarity.

On the weekend of the second anniversary of my dad's death, I got my first tattoo—a semicolon on my right forearm. It is only about an inch long, yet the small indelible mark has created conversations, whether it is someone asking what it means, or another saying, "I understand." What resonated with me was Amy's idea that, whatever our stories are, depression and other mental illnesses are not the end of the sentence. Many of the stories on the website are of people who have survived suicide attempts. The community that has grown because of the website and related programs has helped countless people to keep writing their stories. Had my grandmother still been alive, she probably would have gone with me to get a semicolon tattoo of her own.

My depression has not caused me to seriously ponder suicide, for reasons I understand and others that I don't. The metaphor of the punctuation, however, has marked my life. My depression is a significant break, but it is not a full stop.

In *Noonday Demon: An Atlas of Depression*, Andrew Solomon writes, "It is not an easy diagnosis because it depends on metaphors, and the metaphors one patient chooses are different from those selected by another patient."

One of most enduring metaphors for my depression is I feel like I am chasing the closing circle of light at the end of an old movie, and doing all I can to keep it from going to a total blank screen. I feel frantic and without energy at the same time. The metaphor is about not being enough, not being of value: I can't get to the light, and I don't matter enough for it to wait for me. Ginger reminded me how often I say depression feels like I have a refrigerator on my back. I also say it feels like I'm swimming in molasses, or living in a dull haze—not a fog, because to me, that implies a lack of awareness, which is not accurate. When I feel depressed, I am aware of how dull things are, or all I cannot see.

Depression is an empty stop, rather than a full one. It is a cousin to the crushing certitude of cynicism that offers no sense of uncertainty or bewilderment. It leaves no room for hope. It is suspension in an aching emptiness full of vacant certainty that offers no sense of an ending, and no chance for change. It feels like there is nothing left to say.

When it comes to metaphors, it is hard for me to think of depression as something other than dark—but not dark like the rich array of skin tones that make up humanity. Dark like a moonless night where I can't see beyond the end of my nose. My limited understanding of astronomy helps me to lean into the metaphor of darkness to find more than negative images. A black hole is not only dark, but has a gravitational pull. Its darkness is not a void. A black hole is not empty, not merely the lack of something. It has gravity because it has substance. If you are someone who does not live with depression, understand that it is a weight, a force. It is something that demands a response, even as it saps the energy to respond. It is not something to be solved. It has no a solution.

Depression is isolating and discouraging. What matters most is finding some way to not feel disconnected—to not feel fragmented. A fragment, by definition, is incomplete. When it comes to sentences, the fragment is made more coherent by either adding words or changing the punctuation.

For most of human history, we did not name depression as we do now. The diagnosis is about a hundred years old, so if I go looking for Bible stories about depression, there aren't any, and yet there are. John's gospel holds the story of a man who was ill and had come to the pool at Bethesda every day for thirty-eight years, hoping to be healed—that's all the detail we get. Sometime during the day, an angel "disturbed" the waters, and whoever got in the pool first was healed. For almost fourteen thousand days, he had shown up to try and get to the water first, even though he knew it would never happen. Someone was always faster, or someone had help, or someone was in a better position to make it to the water first. He was never that someone.

I have no reason to claim he was suffering with depression other than the circumstances I just described, which will carry the metaphor. He had lived in the despair of certain defeat for almost forty years. His story was the same day after day. Whatever hope he might have reached for stayed just beyond his reach. Maybe he kept showing up because to succumb to the hopelessness was a death sentence, so he did what he could. Maybe there wasn't anywhere else to go. Maybe he was looking for someone to feel sorry for him, or he found some strange sense of community surrounded by others who never got well, even though he never asked for help.

We are not told how Jesus found him, only that, when he did, Jesus said to him, "Do you want to get well?"

It's that question that gives me eyes to see the man as a metaphor for depression. I picture the man living the same day over and over again. His life had become a series of short sentences, or perhaps the same sentence repeated, the way a middle schooler writes lines over and over on the blackboard during detention. The only punctuation marks he knew were full stops, one after another.

The gospel story doesn't give us enough details to even infer Jesus' tone of voice. Most of the sermons I have heard over the years, and a couple I have preached, make Jesus sound like a therapist, pressing the man to see his role in his futility. He knew trying to get in the pool didn't work, and yet he kept doing it because he couldn't see any other way. But if he really wanted to get well, then Jesus had something he could work with.

As I have come to terms with the reality that depression is something I live with, regardless of circumstance, I have come to this story looking for kindness in Jesus' voice, a kindness I crave, and I hear the question as an invitation for the man to feel something other than despair. Do you want to get well? Yes, you're sick. Yes, the pool offers a chance for healing, but what if there were another way to tell your story? Do you want to get well?

"Sir," the man replied, "I don't have anybody to help me in the water, and someone always gets there first."

The man was not the only one at the pool who came up empty day after day. There was a crowd. Even people with strategies and helpers didn't make it to the water in time. You would think the angel would have splashed around for several minutes just to let a few others have a chance. Once a day must have felt like a parlor trick or some sort of cosmic lottery.

The man was not alone in his despair or sense of failure, which makes me wonder if any sort of community developed around the pool. Was it a selfish free-for-all, or did those who knew they couldn't get to the water first gather together to share their pain? Did anyone help others to move? Did any who were healed ever come back to lend a hand? How many of them were listening in as Jesus said, "Pick up your things and walk"?

The story said the man did what Jesus said and he was healed. Over the nearly twenty years that I have been consciously aware of my depression, healing has had different faces. I have had many years when I have taken medication, and a few that I have not. I have learned to ask for antidepressants when I need them, and they have helped. I have spent a lot of time in therapy, and I am glad I did. These days, I see a spiritual director because I want to learn again to tell the story of the depression and the rest of my life with a vocabulary of faith different from the one I grew up with that said illness was caused by sin, or that if I were to just "get right" with God, I wouldn't be depressed.

Depression is a mental illness, not an indicator that I have done something wrong. I have also been told that God "gave" me my depression so God could be glorified in my healing. I am more than a stage prop for my Creator.

Jesus' encounter with the man at the pool, along with everyone else he talked to, tells me that love is what re-punctuates our lives and helps us see beyond the full stops to replace them. Jesus used a lot of semicolons.

The most punctuating presence in my life continues to be Ginger, who has incarnated that same kind of tenacious and unconditional love every day of our journey together for over thirty years. Her love, along with love from others, has helped me feel like I want to get well, which is not the same as not having to live with the depression. Getting well—feeling whole—has a great deal to do with seeing there is more to me than this one sentence.

One of the things that got lost in the transition from Judaism to Christianity is the sense of looking at a person as a unity of things rather than a collection of compartments. The Shema says, "Love the Lord your God with all your heart, soul, and mind," but does not see each as a separate category or separate from the physical body. The influence of the Greeks gave us centuries of categorizing spiritual as separate from physical, when the truth is found, once again, in the swirl of relationship between body, mind, and spirit.

In learning to live with and through my depression, I have come up against such a separation in my treatment, dividing chemical therapy from talk therapy, as though they were somehow independent of one another. Recent findings about the ways our brains work led me back to what the Hebrews already knew: we are a unity, not a conglomeration of separate things.

I inherited some heart issues from my parents, one of which is atrial fibrillation (a-fib), which means my heart beats more like the extended drum solo from Iron Butterfly's "Inagadadavida," than the iambic pentameter of a sinus rhythm. I have twice undergone a procedure called cardioversion to shock my heart back into rhythm. What I learned from my cardiologist is that there is a relationship between a-fib and depression. A psychologist later told me it works both ways: people with a-fib are more likely to be depressed, and people who are depressed are more likely to have a-fib. A-fibbers are also more likely to have sleep apnea, and vice versa.

I know all three persons of this twisted trinity all too well. The relationship between them is more profound than cause and effect. Snapping my heart back into sinus rhythm doesn't relieve my depression any more than a beautiful afternoon wipes away my grief. However, making changes creates possibilities, even uncertainties; that things do not stay the same gives me hope.

My inherited conditions and the connections between them help remind me that my depression is not my fault. It is not a statement of deficiency on my part any more than my propensity for high blood pressure. Both are part of the unity of body, mind, and spirit, which make me who I am. The call for me is to embrace that complexity as I learn how to be me and become me. I can't deal with my depression on my own, nor can I deal with it as a singular problem independent of circumstance and context. Just as I need to remind myself that I am a unity, so I must remember that I exist in the context of relationships, both with other humans and with the God in whose image we are created.

Depression is not the same thing as sadness or grief. Andrew Solomon says, "Grief is depression in proportion to circumstance; depression is grief out of proportion to circumstance."

When I was teaching at Charlestown High School in Boston, and before my depression had a name or I understood how it was marking my life, Ginger would say, "I think you're depressed," and I would reply, "Life is depressing; this is an appropriate response." I was both right and wrong. There was more going on than responding to my circumstances, and I could not see it. Life was difficult at that time. I was sad, even angry, about my situation. When people asked about my job, I would say, "I feel like every day when I go into the building, part of me dies, and

I come home every night and try to bring it back to life, but I never quite get it all back."

Life has depressing moments, and depression is a mental illness that leaves us pressed down, pressed on, or just pressed. The physical image of a depression is an indentation, a lower place. Meteorologically, a depression is a storm in the tropics, at the beach—even when life seems good, the storm is present—a foreboding gray that haunts the horizon: a heavy absence, a without, an isolation. Like an island after a hurricane, you feel cut off. Without power. Without a way of seeing.

A year and a half after I left Charlestown to teach in Winchester, Massachusetts, I was diagnosed with sleep apnea and began using a CPAP machine. I had always thought I only needed four hours of sleep because it did not feel different to sleep eight hours. After only a couple nights, I realized I had spent most of my life not knowing what rest felt like. It felt wonderful, and once my sleep deprivation was answered, it unmasked the depression underneath it, much like an art restorationist finds a painting under a painting. At first, it felt like a free fall—an ambush—but when I look back, I can see it was more of an uncovering. Once I knew what I was looking for, I was able to see that depression was in me when I was a teenager and a young adult. Now I am in my sixties, and it has risen up with new power.

William Styron titled his book chronicling his depression, *Darkness Visible*. Over the years, I have often used weight as my primary image: an elephant sitting on my chest, a refrigerator on my back, or walking around in a lead suit. I have learned it matters to talk about it because people seem to find resonance, but I am under no illusion that there is only one way to look at or experience depression, any more than there is one way to punctuate a complex sentence. We each see it differently, even as we see the same thing, which means we must consciously choose to not make it a matter of comparison. The chance we have to find strains of grace and hope and love—even gratitude—comes in solidarity and the sharing of our stories, not in the measuring of them one against the other.

One of the metaphors I had to let go of to survive was that of a battle or a fight. I am not saying it is not a valid metaphor, just that it does not work for me. The imagery of war does not speak to me on any level because it implies that responding to violence with violence is a viable solution. That may work in the short term, but violence never solves itself. And depression is violence.

I said earlier that I learned grief was not something to get over, but something to live in the middle of. I am learning that depression is much the same. I live in the middle of my mental illness in the same way I live with my high blood pressure and a-fib. I cannot fight my brain chemistry any more than I can explain it. Some write about learning to see it as a friend, but I am not there yet. I can see it as a fellow traveler, perhaps, which does not necessarily mean I have learned to love it. One image I found years ago was that of *riding the monster*, climbing up on it and seeing where it takes me. The mental picture for me is that guy from *The Neverending Story,* riding the back of the flying beast.

I have not found one metaphor that speaks definitively because I live in the middle of it. I keep adding to my list. The images that are meaningful are relational, dynamic, and—therefore—hopeful. Uncertain. The possibility of a door.

However it feels today, it will not always feel like this.

Depression is not a full stop.

ELLIPSES OF POSSIBILITY

ON THE PAGE, AN ELLIPSIS LOOKS like three periods in a row. Full stop. Full stop. Full stop. Together they become steppingstones across what is missing to connect to what follows...

Here, then, is another metaphor of relationship. Though individually they are stop signs, the three periods together create a waiting room, a pregnant pause that marks the presence of an absence: something left out, something left behind, perhaps something just left. I think they also create a place for what might have been. They make room for what fell away, what has gone missing, or what might happen.

In one of the gospel stories that follow Jesus' resurrection, Luke tells of two men who were walking from Jerusalem, back to their home in Emmaus, towards the end of the same day that Mary Magdalene had mistaken Jesus for the gardener. The two show up nowhere else in scripture, and only one of them is named—Cleopas. They were about seven miles out of town when Jesus joined them on the road, but they did not recognize him. They were not even looking for him. He asked what they had been doing in the city, and they were surprised that he knew nothing of what had transpired. The two men told him all about the Crucifixion and the women's claim that the tomb was empty, and then they said, "But we had hoped that he was the one to redeem Israel."

We had hoped...

Though neither Luke nor most of his translators include the ellipsis (or any other punctuation), I see it when I read the story.

We had hoped...

We set our lives on something that did not roll out the way we planned. Where we thought there would be something, instead there is an absence we do not know how to engage. An uncertainty. Once again, we are reading a story grounded in grief.

The story gets more interesting because Jesus let them keep talking, without interrupting to say, "Hey, it's me!" He kept walking and listening until they got to Emmaus, and then he acted as though he still had miles to go. They insisted he stay for dinner, so he did. When he broke the bread and blessed it, they recognized him, and Luke says he disappeared. They got up and ran the miles back to tell their friends in Jerusalem. Then they disappeared from the pages of scripture.

What I love most about this story is, though things had not played out in Jerusalem as they expected, the men kept going. They had hoped and they had been disappointed, but they did not despair. They were grieving, but they were still willing to talk about it. They were willing to be bewildered by their circumstances. They kept walking together and telling their story. The road back to Emmaus was an ellipsis—room to see what would fill what had fallen away—and Jesus met them there, which sent them running back to their friends in the middle of the Palestinian night.

I am more accustomed to the gray and cold of a New England winter than the heat of a desert evening. Even more, I have come to love the spirit that rises up in people when we have a winter storm. However heavy the snow might fall, as soon as we can, we are digging out and getting on with our lives. It doesn't matter how high the parking lot mountains get, we shovel our walks, clean off our cars, dress in layers, and keep on living. Neither the storm nor the aftermath gets the last word.

During one of the blizzards that hit the winter after we moved into our row house in Charlestown, I joined our neighbors to dig out our cars. None of us had garages, and our street was a one-way dead-end street, which meant it didn't get plowed. We had a good foot of snow on the ground, the street, the sidewalks, and the cars. As soon as someone finished their car, they moved over to help the person next to them. An elderly couple lived on the block, and some moved to shovel the sidewalk in front of their house. If we needed a break, we took it, but the point was to stay out there until everyone's car was accessible and our street was clear. We were in it together.

What moves me most about my faith is the Incarnation: God with us and in us, as one of us. Jesus' words and actions are more viscerally hopeful than any promise of a heaven to be named later. If Jesus had been born in New England, he would have been out shoveling with the rest of us. Yes, he told his disciples of mansions to come, but he spent more time talking to them about forgiving one another, about living out love in practical and uncomfortable ways, about speaking truth to power and helping marginalized people feel like they belong. Jesus never encouraged anyone to lose hope in the present moment. He knew life was messy and hard and as relentless as the weather, and that the hopes and fears of all the years showed up on a daily basis. He talked about hope like it mattered for the poor and the meek and the mourning who were digging out of their lives and going on together. And he knew the only way to live was to spend it all—spend the grief and the grace, spend the sadness and the heartache, spend the compassion and the camaraderie. His ministry lasted three years—an ellipsis in human history.

As I talk about Jesus' life as an ellipsis, I realize that I have moved back and forth between singular and plural in describing the metaphor. An ellipsis is made up of three periods: it or they? The three full stops take on a collective presence, much like we talked about the Trinity as both singular and collective. An ellipsis is relational punctuation—a way we give pause to one another and create room for uncertainty and bewilderment.

"Hope, like faith" Thornton Wilder wrote, "is nothing if it is not courageous; it is nothing if it is not ridiculous." Hope is being able to see an ellipsis and not just a string of cynical full stops. Hope, also, may best take root when we don't pin everything on being right.

We have a sign hanging in our barn that says, "Be kind because everyone you meet is fighting a great battle." I first heard those words in a sermon Ginger preached, which is the reason we bought the sign. The saying goes back to antiquity, as does grief. In one of my jobs, part of our training was to learn to "assume positive intent" in our dealing with other people, both customers and fellow employees. More recently, in discussions centered around white male privilege, I learned a helpful acrostic for an extrovert like me: WAIT—Why Am I Talking?

I would love to say my life is filled with stories of lived ellipses, but—beyond punctuation—I am still learning how to write sentences that have fewer quotes from me, and more from those whose lives had led them to different questions than the ones I learned to ask. I found one anonymous quote that said an ellipsis is like an open window. A breath of fresh air. An invitation for something new to come flying in.

The two walking with Jesus on the road to Emmaus couldn't quit talking long enough to pay attention to who was with them. Jesus walked along and listened. They recognized him when they became quiet enough to see beyond the full stop of their grief and disappointment.

The less I talk, and the more I wait and listen...the more hopeful my life becomes.

SPACE FOR CREATING

MY NEPHEWS BEN AND SCOTT began playing soccer as little boys. The youngest one, Scott, was on a team of five-year-olds that dominated their league because of how their coach taught them to play. Beginning soccer is gang ball for the most part. The children are magnetically attracted to the ball and move in a big lump, up and down the field. Scott's coach had one instruction: Run to the open space. To run away from the ball created possibility. Run to the open space and let the ball come to you.

Space as a metaphor of possibility has had a long-standing meaning in my life, but as I tell the story alongside these other metaphors of punctuation, it carries me to a different place—or I suppose I could say, to a different space. When I was learning to type, one of the first rules I remember was that there was one space between words, and two spaces at the end of a sentence. After a period, there was more room. The rule was not arbitrary; the extra space made the page more readable. As we have moved from typewriters to laptops, the word processing programs space things in such a way that the double space is no longer suggested, for the most part, yet there remains a vigorous group of folks who champion the small expansion. I can see their point. We all need a little more space to come to terms with the endings in our lives, and maybe the middles and beginnings as well.

I wonder if space is becoming a diminished metaphor in these days of smartphones and constant connectivity, which is not necessarily the same thing as intentional connectedness. When I go into New York, I have about a ten-minute walk from Grand Central to my office. I make a conscious choice to not take my phone out while I am walking, mostly so I don't walk into anyone. I am in the minority on the sidewalks of Madison Avenue in doing so. The space between the station and my building offers me a chance to notice the way the morning light lays across the tops of the buildings, to smile at babies in strollers and puppies sniffing every flower bed, or to just take in the array of humanity that walks by me, if I am paying attention. The space on the sidewalk reminds me that urgent and important are not always synonyms; life without space quickly drains of meaning. Space makes room for all kinds of good things—and space is what we have to cross to connect with one another.

Earlier I quoted John Berger saying hope was "measuring distances and walking toward." He used the word *approach*, which has its roots in ecclesiastical Latin, which is to say it began as a church word. It means to draw near. Approaching makes me think of walking up to the altar for communion: standing in the unbroken line of saints who have come before us, who point us to the horizon even as we feel the push of those who will come after us, expecting the path of discipleship to remain well-worn. I can also see how we move toward one another in the communion ritual, where we pass the plates down the pews, offering and receiving, approaching one another in the name of Christ, reaching out as we give and take. Approach: the peace of Christ be with you; and also with you.

"Teach us to number our days," were words from Psalm 90 that we considered at the beginning of this book. Teach us to measure our distances might be another way to say it. We measure forty days from Ash Wednesday to Easter, not counting Sundays, even as we also number the days of Advent, Christmastide, Eastertide, and Ordinary Time. God has shown us how far it is to forgiveness, how closely grace resides, how long and wide and deep and high the love of Christ truly is. We measure distance—space—to know what we need to do to get to one another. Then we walk towards. We approach.

Another word for space is room. On the page, space is what lies in between the top of the page, and where the type begins; the end of a chapter and the start of the next. We put space between words and between sentences so they make sense to us. Space is room to move, room to pause. Just room. It is there to help words make sense. Space helps define the relationships between everything else on the page. But beyond punctuation, space is what we stare into at night when we look up into the stars. It is what we hope for when we sit on a train or a plane. It is the distance from there to here.

The first notes I have on this book go back to late 2015, a little over two years after my father died. That you are reading this page means he has been dead over seven years. Every book has a longer-than-expected gestation period, I assume, but this one was lengthened by a lack of space. Our move to Guilford meant that I lost my office—my writing room. I tried taking up residence at one end of the dining table, but any number of things meant I had to keep moving my stuff, which also became an excuse for not writing. As I pushed my publication deadline back again and again, I kept trying to figure out how to finish the book.

Walking home one day, I passed a sign for Guilford Co-Working. I wrote an email inquiry and found there was room for me to have a dedicated writing space. I was protective of it.

I didn't edit there. I didn't blog or pay bills there. I wrote. What had floundered for three years came alive once I ran to the open space.

One word I can use to talk about the writing space as I have described it, is sacred, as in set apart for a specific purpose. In the same way, our barn is sacred space because we have set it aside as the place to gather around our big table and share meals. Sacred carries a spiritual connotation: set apart for something beyond ourselves. Church sanctuaries, cemeteries, and memorials are sacred spaces. Holy ground.

The first few months of the pandemic took away all the sacred spaces I just named. Because it was a co-working site, I couldn't use my writing space. Because of the quarantine and physical distancing, we couldn't host barn dinners, nor could we gather for worship in the sanctuary. So much of our holy ground was cordoned off. To both finish the book and do my daily work, I had to learn how to make space at the end of the dining table instead of running to an open field or another building. I had to make room in the space I already inhabited.

In one sense, we are surrounded by space. In another, our environments are made up of all kinds of spaces. We have to make room for ourselves and for what matters.

Space is a time word as well, meaning an interval, like time between trains. In the same way life is a collection of physical spaces, it is a collection of intervals and in-betweens.

Perhaps when we learn to live and rest in those intervals, they become sacred—places where we can be made whole.

THE LONG
TABLE OF
COMPANIONSHIP

WITH BREAD

IN EVERY TOWN GINGER AND I have lived, gathering people around our dinner table has been a central part of our life together. In our Boston neighborhood of Charlestown, we shoehorned our handmade table into the dining room of our little row house, and fed as many as we could fit. In our house by the sea in Marshfield, dinner often meant a walk down to the water afterwards. In Durham, our house on West Trinity Avenue was an invitation made of wood, brick, and mortar. We had room to add tables, or to move out on the big porch to share a meal on Thursday nights. In Guilford, we turned the old barn behind our house into a gathering place, and now our barn dinners gather people around a thirteen-foot long table, built by Mark, our church sexton.

Rumi wrote,

> just beyond the arguing
>
> there is a long table of companionship
>
> set and waiting for us to sit down.

Perhaps all of our tables have sat just beyond arguing, but they have also sat in the middle of our griefs, our joys, in our comings and goings—all the changes that make up what we call life. Every time I see the meme that says, "When you have more than you need, build a longer table, not a higher wall," I think of our Thursday night dinners.

Rumi also wrote,

> Out beyond ideas of wrongdoing
> and rightdoing there is a field.
> I'll meet you there.

Something about things that were *beyond* pulled him. Beyond arguing. Beyond ideas, which, I suppose, could be close to the same thing. Out beyond our head games, our wish to be right, there is a table, a field, a place where we can lay it all down together.

The root words of companion mean *with bread*. We build relationships at the table. We make memories at the table. We set places and note absences, we welcome, and we bid farewell— all at the table. When someone dies, we show up at the house with food. We come to be companions. Our casseroles and covered dishes are tangible and tasty ways of showing that love is shared loss. Beyond our differing perspectives, beyond our disagreements, there is a place to be together and share our sorrow while we share a meal.

Our foremost family companions, if I take the word at its roots, are Ben and Jenny, our nephew and niece-in-law who live in New Orleans. Ben is a pastor, and Jenny is a doctor in a public health clinic. When we are together, we eat and we enjoy it. For our wedding anniversary one year, they took us to La Petite Grocery, and I had one of the best meals of my life. The next day, we devoured five or six dozen oysters at Superior Seafood. When we are together, we are with each other and we are with bread—

and wine, and oysters, and whatever else we can think of. Every meal is a celebration.

One of the stories Jesus told is one we have come to call the Parable of the Great Banquet. A host wanted to throw a big party, so they sent invitations to their usual circle of rich friends, but everyone answered with an excuse for why they couldn't come, most of which were of the I-have-to-polish-my-bowling-ball variety. They assumed the hospitality of the host would still be available when it was more convenient for them. Such is the logic of privilege. The host sent their servants out to find anyone who was hungry enough to come to dinner, telling them to find people wherever they could. Everyone was invited.

The interpretation I heard most often growing up was that God was the host, and we were either the servants or the reluctant invitees, but that doesn't add up. God doesn't give people of privilege the first right of refusal and then turn to the *others*. Rather than being a metaphor for God, perhaps the host is the one with something to learn in this story. Those who think it is *just another dinner* aren't the ones who will feed our hearts and truly share the table. Find the people who are hungry and want to eat. Don't just tell them the food is here, bring them home with you. Share your losses, even as you share the meal, and everyone will be nourished.

Friendships are more than invitations. They are creative acts of intention—or perhaps, intentional acts of creation—that require courage, compassion, and even insistence. To create a relationship is to build something out of the suggestion of a connection. True connections have layers and layers of stories, like the paint on an icon, or the sheet upon sheet of buttered phyllo dough that becomes baklava.

My friends Elizabeth and Roberto own COPA, a Cuban restaurant in Durham, that is the first farm-to-table Cuban restaurant in the country. They also have a farm, Terra Sacra, where they grow a good deal of their produce. They have been intentional about forging relationships with the farmers that raise the pigs and chickens they need for their dishes. You can taste the intentionality in everything. They say their mission statement is "cultivating relationships"—with the soil, the produce, the animals, their suppliers, their staff, their customers. The long table of companionship runs from the farm to their friends, to the kitchen that makes the dishes that feed friends gathered in their restaurants to make memories.

"O taste and see that the Lord is good," sang the psalmist in the middle of Psalm 34, a hymn that runs the gamut of emotions. Regardless of circumstance, there is something that connects us at the table. We create, we are nourished, we are together.

The Latin root of intention means to *stretch toward*, another way of describing the action of approach. To live with intention is to stretch toward wholeness, toward grace, toward connection, toward excellence, toward love. It is to measure the distance and then do what it takes to get there.

My friend Claudia is an artist and graphic designer in Durham. When I lived there, we met monthly for lunch. Besides eating and catching up, we met to spur each other on artistically. She brought some sort of drawing or painting, and I brought a poem. She then went home and painted whatever she saw in my poem, and I wrote about what I found in her painting. We never did anything with our art beyond offering and exchanging. Though we never said it out loud, I think we both realized it was the doing of the thing together that gave it value, not the chances of it being a book or an exhibit. Our monthly meal was its own table of companionship that has kept us connected even though we now live in different states.

Long can carry a sense of time, as in how long we've known each other. Relationships that matter are ones with histories that hold stories of love lived out, pain endured, forgiveness offered and received, and lots of food.

A great deal of the important events in Jesus' life included meals. Many of his encounters happened around a table, not the least of which was the Last Supper, on the night before he was executed. As Christians, we serve the bread and wine to one another at communion as a testament to the long table of companionship that runs through our faith, and includes all those who came before us and all who will follow. But there's one meal I think we pass by too quickly. It happened after the Resurrection, in the same time frame as Jesus' walk with those on the Emmaus Road. And Jesus did something he had not done before: he cooked. He carried out his earthly ministry, endured the cross and the grave, came back from the dead, and made breakfast. I love that.

The disciples and the others had not yet made sense of life after Jesus' death, even though some had seen the Risen Christ, the Resurrection had not erased the grief. They were all indelibly marked by the Crucifixion and all that had happened around it. Judas was dead. Peter still carried the weight of his denial. There was Before; this was After. They had the memory of their last supper with Jesus, but things had not been right since, so they went fishing. They went back to what they knew how to do, hoping something would make sense.

They fished all night and had nothing to show for it as the sun was coming up. Their futility must have been excruciating. Things were broken, and they couldn't be fixed. Life was never going to be like it was before. Then they heard a voice call out from the shore, asking if they had caught anything. They reported their failure, and the person told them to cast the net on the right side of the boat. They had nothing to lose, so they followed the instructions that came out of the fading darkness, and came up with a net so full it almost sank them.

Peter said, "It's Jesus," dropped his net, and swam to shore, where he found Jesus cooking fish on the beach, over an open fire. Maybe it mattered that the last time he had stood around a charcoal fire had been in the courtyard, denying he had anything to do with Jesus. Or perhaps he had been around one of those fires every day since. Maybe it mattered that Jesus served bread and fish, much like the lunch the little boy had offered when they ended up feeding over five thousand people and had baskets and baskets of leftovers. Or perhaps they ate fish at most every meal. Maybe it mattered that Jesus asked Peter if he loved him three times—as many times as Peter had betrayed him. Or perhaps it mattered, mostly, that Jesus made breakfast and fed the friend who had disowned him, offering him the grace to know his betrayal was not the last word, and to know that there was something beyond the courtyard, the cross, and the cemetery, even beyond the fretful night they had just lived through.

In the first couple hundred years after Jesus, the communities of faith gathered around a meal. The shared supper was less like the silver trays we pass, and a lot more like the potluck meals congregations or neighbors share from time to time. They told old stories, new stories, and remembered—they put themselves back together again in Jesus' name, much like Jesus did with Peter and those gathered around the fire that morning. Paul even wrote to the church in Corinth and said, *If you have something wrong between you and someone else, make it right before you come to the table.* Give yourself a story to tell.

Though pretty much every one of the disciples bailed out in one way or another when Jesus was arrested, the two that get the spotlight are Peter and Judas, the denier and the betrayer. Those are harsh labels. I don't think either one was malicious in their actions. Peter was in the courtyard because he was trying to stay close to Jesus, and he outran his courage. I think Judas expected Jesus to take on the oppressive government, and was trying to force Jesus' hand and make him act. The biggest difference between the two is Judas never made it to breakfast. If he had, there would have been forgiveness for him as well.

To come to the table together—any table—is to incarnate hospitality and move beyond the hypothetical into actual contact and connection. To share a meal is to risk talking with your mouth full or spilling something on your shirt. It is also to risk staying at the table long after you have finished eating, and begin telling the stories that take a while to come to the surface.

Each time Jesus asked Peter, "Do you love me?" and Peter replied, "Yes, Lord," Jesus said, "Feed my sheep," leaning into a metaphor Jesus used throughout his ministry. What I hear in his words is, *You know what it feels like to completely screw up. You know what it feels like to feel hungry for hope. You know what it feels like to be fed by grace and to be loved back into being. Go find the others who know how you feel, and bring them to dinner—to the extended table.*

Our church in Guilford celebrated our 375th anniversary in 2018. I won't make you do the math; we were founded in 1643, just four years after the first families arrived. The founding families signed a covenant, which is memorialized on a large granite tablet that rests not far from the old stone house where the first pastor lived. They promised to:

> ...sit down and join ourselves together in one entire plantation and to be helpful to each to other in any common work, according to every [one's] ability and as need shall require, and we promise not to desert or leave each other or the plantation, but with the consent of the rest, or the greater part of the company who have entered into this engagement.

They promised no one would leave without the others agreeing. They knew they needed the companionship to survive. I don't think those who first gathered almost four centuries ago could have imagined who we have become as both a town and a congregation. There are instances in our history when the congregation split. I would guess there were times when they wondered how they would keep going. And yet here we are. And we got from there to here by living day to day. Yes, along the way, people planned and saved and worked and created. Yes, along the way, they began to think of ways to provide for those who came after them, but they could not see the future, and so we have ended up with things like an endowed fund to buy hats for the minister's wife. (True story.)

When Jesus shared the bread and the wine with his disciples, I'm not sure he knew he was instituting a ritual for all to follow, as much as saying, "Every time you eat, remember me." He was taking care of his friends on that particular night. He was giving them food for that day. The next morning, they would need to eat again. A meal is not intended to leave us filled forever. Here we are, down all the days, still being fed by God, and feeding one another in a ritual of dependence, trust, and generosity.

One of the ways Ginger and I have built our marriage is in making big deals out of birthdays and anniversaries. Birthdays mean looking for something to do that we have not done before. One year, when we lived in Durham, she drove me down roads I had never seen. As we drove, she would intermittently start laughing and say, "This may be the craziest thing I've ever taken you to do." We ended up in downtown Zebulon, North Carolina.

I was looking for 410 West Gannon Street. As we drove, I saw the Family Dollar, the Dollar General, the Dollar Tree. When the GPS said we had reached our destination, we were in the parking lot of the Piggly Wiggly. We had driven an hour to join in the celebration of the store's second anniversary. Ginger had heard it advertised on her drive home from Charlotte the previous week.

A big Trailways type bus tricked-out to advertise North Carolina agriculture was parked in front of the store, as was a giant grocery cart that had an engine in it. A local radio station was giving away all kinds of swag, alongside a fire truck. Two food tents offered free hot dogs and ham biscuits, and a refrigerated eighteen-wheeler was decorated with a *Truckload of Meat Deals* banner down the side. Inside the store, people stood at the end of almost every aisle, with some sort of barbecued meat or sauce. It was worth the drive.

The assistant store manager was standing on the back of the meat truck when we walked up. He greeted us and gave us a tour of what was inside, and told us about the store and their plans for the day. His pride and enthusiasm were contagious. Inside the store, which still seemed shiny and new, the staff was engaging. They were fascinated that we had driven up from Durham to take part in the festivities, and they were happy to include us in what was mostly a hometown happening.

After we finished at the store, Ginger and I walked across the street to the Old Town Cafe. As we drank our coffee, I said, "There's something wonderful about a town small enough to make a big deal about a grocery store's birthday." As the day went on, my words circled back, and I realized those kinds of personal connections are what matter most, regardless of how big the town is. That's how you fill a long table.

While we lived in Durham, we celebrated the opening of Cocoa Cinnamon, the world's best coffee shop, and stood in line the first morning that Monuts, our favorite donut shop, opened their first restaurant. In Charlestown, we walked down to Collier's Market for the world's greatest cheeseburger sub. In Guilford, we marked the eightieth anniversary of Page's Hardware, even as we said goodbye to the Sunny Side Up Café, our favorite breakfast place.

As we celebrate openings and anniversaries, and grieve closings and goodbyes that matter only to us, we build the long table of companionship that connects to tables in other towns and communities where the stories are different, and still the same.

We are our version of Zebulon, wherever we are, gathered with loved ones and sharing in seeing their dreams come true.

PREPARING

IN ENGLISH CLASS, I LEARNED that a metaphor states that one thing is another thing, like singing, "A mighty fortress is our God." Literally, God is more than bricks and battlements, and the line is true.

The power of a metaphor, often, is the distance between the two things. *Life is a box of chocolates* works because the contrast is stark. Life doesn't fit in a box, for a start. When it comes to looking at all we do around and with food as metaphor, I face a challenge because much of life is working with and around food, even though I no longer cook for a living. I don't know how to see them as disparate things. And I can hear Ronny Cammareri in *Moonstruck,* saying, "What is life? They say bread is life. And I bake bread. And I sweat and shovel this stinkin' dough in and out of this hot hole in the wall, and I should be so happy! Huh, sweetie?"

Well, sweetie, I am a cook because of my mother. Almost as far back as I remember, I was drawn to the kitchen, and she was loving and opportunistic enough to reel me in. One of the earliest lessons I learned from her about preparing a meal was to work on each dish in such a way that they were all ready at the same time. She was a master. The lessons in her kitchen helped me during my restaurant days, but even more so at home.

To prepare a meal is not to get ready in general, but to aim at a specific moment. In my first book, I said, "Sacredness requires specificity." That's why mealtime matters. You start with the moment in mind and then back up from there. What needs to cook the longest? What requires the most amount of labor? What is not affected by the timeline or can be done ahead? What needs to happen in the moment—at the last minute?

The word *prepare* can mean getting ready, as in setting up a room, making plans, or making something, as in I am preparing your meal. It can also mean being ready, as in, I am prepared for the evening, which is another way of saying, "Bring it on." If the long table of companionship is our metaphor, what are we preparing for? What do we need to get ready? What are we making? What should we have at hand?

I know. I'm asking a lot of questions.

One of my favorite cookbooks is the *Improvisational Cook* by Sally Schneider, because cooking, for her, is all about the questions. She helped learn how to not to rely on a recipe, but to adapt it. Improvising with food is not so different than improvising with music. The big difference for me is I am fluent in the language of cooking in ways I am not when I pick up my guitar. My other favorite cookbook is *Ruhlman's Twenty: 20 Techniques 100 Recipes A Cook's Manifesto* because it is not primarily about recipes. Michael Ruhlman identifies twenty ingredients and techniques that a cook needs to master to give them the skills to be prepared for whatever happens in the kitchen. Since I have spent a fair amount of this book working in threes, I'll give you one more, also by Ruhlman—*Ratio: The Simple Codes Behind the Craft of Everyday Cooking*—in which he breaks down everything from salad dressing to pound cake into ratios, which means you can make enough for two or enough for twenty because you know how the ingredients relate to each other.

One of the joys of summer in a New England garden are the squash blossoms. My restaurant days taught me how to stuff them with seasoned ricotta cheese, batter them, and fry them. They are incredible. I found a recipe for squash blossom quesadillas that involved chopping off the stems and taking out the stamens, and then laying them in a half-circle around one side of a tortilla, along with cheese, and then heating them up in a skillet. As I began to put them together, I looked around for what else I could add to make something I had not thought of before. I had some homemade black-eyed peas and a poblano pepper, which I roasted. I created something that I repeated a couple of times before the blossoms season was over.

Laura Esquivel's novel *Like Water for Chocolate* is subtitled *A Novel in Monthly Installments with Recipes, Romances, and Home Remedies*. Each chapter begins with a recipe that becomes the metaphor for what happens that month. In one sense, it becomes obvious that any recipe we have for life will have to be adapted, if not scrapped. Thus, the need to know about ingredients, techniques, and ratios so we can make the best of what we have. If life gives us lemons, we have more options than just lemonade. What else is in the pantry? What are we hungry for? We may have what we need to make chicken piccata, lemon pound cake, or homemade Limoncello.

When I started cooking for a job, I learned about the *mise en place*, which is French for *everything in its place*. On a restaurant cooking line, each person has their station and they stock it with all the things they will need for dinner service, along with backups of things that will need to be replaced. Taking the time to prepare usually makes for an easier evening, or, if nothing else, allows more ways to respond to the unexpected things the night most assuredly brings.

Some of the places I worked had set menus, but when I managed the restaurant on the Duke University campus, part of the challenge is we got what was left over from the owner's other two places, which meant we had to improvise most every night in one way or another. My favorite was the day we got a container full of red velvet cake edges that had been trimmed for a catering gig. I went to my recipe book and turned the crumbs into red velvet bread pudding, since we had eggs and cream on hand, made a white chocolate sauce to go on top, and we sold out.

Preparing doesn't always mean we get our just desserts. Sometimes the unexpected is tragic and undeserved. Two days after Ginger returned from El Paso, where she had joined a gathering of clergy at the US-Mexico border to protest the detention centers, an angry white man walked into a Walmart, intent on killing people he saw as *invaders*, those who didn't look like him. The store was filled with people shopping for school clothes and supplies. They had no way to be prepared for an angry man intent on doing damage.

We have so many memories of mass shootings across our country that we can see that though there is little protection in the moment, what we are prepared to do in the aftermath is care for one another.

Compassion is one of the ingredients that needs to be in the pantry as we prepare for the table of companionship. Both words begin with *con-*, the Latin prefix which means *with*, which we have already talked about being the most important word in the Bible. With bread; suffering with.

The picture that jumps to mind is the collection of casseroles that show up at a home in the South when someone has died. Sharing a meal is one of the best ways to share our suffering.

As I think about other ingredients for the pantry, I realize this metaphor takes me to many of the same places the porters of punctuation, color, and music did. Kindness. Attention.

Thoughtfulness. Listening. Gratitude. Grace. Perhaps that is why we can talk about tone in music and art and language, and texture in food and song and paint. Preparing is another way of listening, of setting up the *mise en place*, running scales, or tracing lines on an icon. Getting ready for what is to come, or simply facing the day ahead, is more than making a list and checking it twice. The writer of Ephesians described preparation as putting on the armor of God. My father used to say that the preposition *of* was not possessive but descriptive: The armor didn't belong to God; it *was* God.

Dress in God to prepare for what is coming. Paul named the pantry as fruit of the Spirit: love, joy, peace, patience, kindness, goodness, faithfulness, gentleness, and self-control. (Gal. 5:22-23, Common Bible)

From our *mise en place*, we prepare—we make the meal.

Ellen Bass has a poem, "If You Knew," which begins with the question, "What if you knew you'd be the last to touch someone?" Linda Pastan's "Imaginary Conversation" says, "Why not live each day as if it were the first?" We like to think in beginnings and endings, the great start and the finishing flourish, but it is the daily preparation, the daily presentation of our gifts, that make up what matters in life.

In *First You Write a Sentence*, Joe Moran describes the Japanese idea of *shokunin Karachi*, or the artisanal spirit, which is about more than mere skill. "It beats the social obligation to make something for the joy of making it, quietly and beautifully.... The point of life is to infuse the quotidian with the pleasure of creation and the pursuit of perfection."

Apprenticeship is built into Japanese culture. For Americans, not so much. They appear to be a culture of learners. We like to be the experts. It's hard to prepare well if you think you know everything. In every kitchen, I have learned from the people standing on either side of me, whether in restaurants, someone else's home, or in my kitchen. To cook together is to prepare together, and that means to learn together.

The best way to prepare to write is to read. One writer suggested that you spend ten times as much time reading as you do writing if you want to write well. I have never lived up to that ratio, but both in my writing and my editing, reading good sentences helps me prepare for my work. I learn from the ways in which other people put words together, much as I learn from other people who put ingredients together and then share their work.

My father, the Southern Baptist minister, loved to preach. He loved to pastor. He had an opinion on everything. Until Ginger came into his life, he had never had a relationship with a woman who shared his vocational call. I watched her build a relationship with him by calling and saying, "Milton, I'm sure you've dealt with this in your ministry...," and then she would ask him a question or describe a situation. Her reaching out created a mutuality between them that helped him move beyond his need to be the expert. They even began to share sermon ideas.

When I begin to prepare for a barn dinner, I look first at what I have on hand, whether that is something in the fridge that needs to be used, something from the garden, or something in the pantry that calls out to me, like arborio rice or pinto beans. Often, I decide the menu in the aisles of one of the markets in town, as I did when I saw the squash blossoms. Sometimes I begin with the allergies or dietary restrictions of those around the table. For example, Ginger has an onion allergy, which has challenged me to find new ways to add flavor to dishes. My preparation process then shifts to a kind of free association, letting my mind make connections or remember things I had forgotten. The quesadillas set me thinking about Latin flavors, and I remembered a plantain press my friend Jeanette had given me, so I bought plantains as well and looked up a recipe for *tostones rellenos*—stuffed plantains—which became the second course of the meal.

The same kind of things happen when we prepare to take care of each other, to be with each other. Whether we are literal companions who show up with bread and soup, or friends who offer our care in other tangible ways, we have to think about how to put our care into a tangible, or perhaps visceral, form. What do we know about the person who is hurting? What can we offer? What can we say? How can we listen? What have we learned that is ripe for this moment?

To prepare is to make ourselves living metaphors, porters of compassion, pictures of what love is like.

SHARING

IF YOU WERE TO LOOK THROUGH THE PICTURES stored on my phone, you would find an abundance of food photos. I make a point of photographing my Thursday night dinner dishes, but I also take pictures of food served to me when I want to be able to show it to someone else. In my restaurant work, I learned that people taste with their eyes as well as their mouths. Their noses, also. Presentation matters. We were expected to think about how the various elements should go on the plate, or how it would be composed, to borrow an art and music word.

A meal is a work of art. When I am serving food, I think about taste, shape, texture, and color, as well as the effect the items on the plate have on one another. If I want something to be crunchy and I cover it in sauce, I defeat my own purpose. Good chefs will think about the color of the plate as they work on a menu.

But a meal is not art for the ages; it is intentionally temporary art for a particular moment in time. Cooks know we are offering our art, intending for it to be destroyed, like the artist I found on YouTube one afternoon, who builds sculptures next to the ocean so they will be taken out with the tide. He spends hours designing and building things he knows will not survive the waves, and he does it in a way that even their destruction is artful.

Food is to be savored, not saved. Dig in. Enjoy it. Let the temporary become memorable, and brush up against what is durable and eternal. A good meal becomes a thin place to underline that the point of this life is not to last forever, but to be re-membered. Put back together.

Sharing is relishing the temporary, the specificity of the moment. Any gathering at the table, even if the same people are sitting in their assigned places, will be different from any other night because some detail of life—some specific—will be different. Life doesn't show reruns. This is all the time we have. This all that we have. And it is enough to share. Let's make the best of it. To allow a theology of scarcity to feed us a diet of fear and anger is to miss the banquet to which God has invited us all, every last one of us.

To share a meal is to tell a story with both the food and the companionship. When we baked cookies to sell in Durham, we told people we designed the cookies to tell a story that had a beginning, a middle, and an end. You had to wait a few seconds after you bit into the peanut butter chocolate chip sriracha cookie before the heat revealed itself. We introduced our Old North Durham Cookie by saying it was a lot like our neighborhood: it had a little bit of everything.

Walk through any bookstore and you'll see shelves full of biographies. Life stories. Most of them are one-volume works, which means the author spent as much time deciding what to leave out as what to write down. Part of that process is choosing specific situations that are emblematic of the larger life of the person. The moment becomes a metaphor. Instead of saying she was generous, they tell a story of her gift to the children's hospital. Instead of saying he had a temper, they recall a time when he punched a hole in his bedroom wall.

Instead of describing my mother, I will tell you a story. We lived in Lusaka, Zambia, when the country became independent. The days leading up to the official celebration were packed with activities. Lusaka was filled with dignitaries because it was the capital city. My mother was downtown shopping when she saw a number of VIPs entering a building. She walked up to see what was going on, and the guard on duty told her that only invitees and the press were allowed to enter. Without hesitating, she reached in her purse, pulled out her Texas driver's license, showed it to the guard, and said, "I'm with the *Dallas Morning News*." He opened the barrier and let her through.

Her life was filled with stories like that. When she was in hospice, we opened the Bible she had for years and found a list of fifty names in the back. My sister-in-law Ginger asked what they were. My mother replied that they were the names of people she had helped over the years. Both Gingers and my brother and I sat there and listened to her tell stories as we read off the names. A life is made of stories. A life is a story.

I love the image of a life story because that makes us characters who grow and change, rather than thinking of ourselves as hardwired personalities. I understand there's helpful stuff in both metaphors—character or personality—but the story is what speaks to me. Perhaps that is why I have ended up talking about stories when I am supposed to be unpacking the metaphor of sharing at the long table of companionship. For me, to share the table is share a story together.

At our barn dinners, Ginger works hard to encourage people to have one conversation around the table, rather than a bunch of smaller ones. I say Ginger does it because she is the *front of the house* when it comes to dinner. How she sets the table makes a difference. She puts out place cards and decorates the table with place mats, flowers, and candles. Always candles. She spends a good bit of time thinking about how we should all be grouped around the table, making introductions and connections that are often significant. She makes the room an invitation you can walk into. On nights when there are twenty or more around the table, talking as one group is more difficult, but I love the sense that we are aware that we are one around the table, and not a bunch of singles at a lunch counter. We are sharing our moment at the long table of companionship.

Thinking about the barn dinners takes me back to the parable of the Great Banquet. I wonder if the host had had dinners before and the original invitees were ones who were used to coming, or if he was trying something new. He seemed to have both the venue and the staff to pull off the party. Perhaps the unflattering refusals caused an identity crisis for him. To throw a dinner party is to invite people into your story. Come to our house. Come eat our food. Sit at our table. When no one wanted to hear that story, maybe he had to ask himself whose story he was trying to tell. Was the point for everyone to be impressed with dinner—and thus, with him—or was the story about feeding people. When he realized it was not his story, and he was sharing in a larger one, he sent his people out to find whoever was hungry to come and eat.

The story of sharing the table involves us all, whether we are the hosts or the hungry ones.

CLEANING UP

HOWARD THURMAN'S POEM "The Work of Christmas," says that work begins after the cast of characters gathered around the crèche have gone home. The last line of the poem says the work of Christmas is "to make music in the heart." After the big event is over, sing your way into cleaning up and moving on.

Cleanup is not a favorite for most of us, and perhaps not something we automatically think of as part of what it means to meet at the table. The kitchen can be a mess.

My first forays into cooking on my own began my junior year in college when I moved out of the dorm and into an apartment. My roommate didn't cook, and loved to eat. He agreed to cleanup if I would make the meals. I remember the first time I made fried chicken. My mother was on the phone coaching me on how to put the chicken in the flour and then the egg wash and then back in the flour. It came out pretty well. When we sat down to dinner, the kitchen looked as though I had opened a five-pound bag of flour, grabbed it by the bottom, and flung it around. That was one night I didn't make my roommate cleanup by himself.

These days, I make a point to try and clean as I go, but that doesn't always happen. Depending on how adventurous I've been, or what surprises came up as I was preparing, the kitchen can be a mess by the time dinner is ready to serve. Even when all goes well, we always have plates and silverware to clear, place mats and napkins to wash, and wine bottles to rinse and recycle. Cleanup is part of the deal.

In restaurants, the last thing to do before leaving the kitchen is to clean. *Well.* After a busy night, it can feel laborious, but it is one way to limit the number of pests that come looking for food, and certainly a way to avoid the ire of co-workers who have the lunch shift the next day. Cleanup is paying it forward, once again understanding that we are a part of a larger story. It is not something to leave for someone else.

In every place we have had our dinners, people have asked how they can help cleanup. They don't just eat and leave. It took a while for me to learn to accept their offer and understand that the work of art that is dinner together isn't over until we have put away our art supplies, cleaned the countertops, and washed the dishes. Cleaning up is part of it, not something that happens afterward. Some of my favorite conversations have happened over cleanup, in the closing moments of an evening together.

I think again of Jesus' encounter with Peter on the beach after Peter's denial, and I realize that forgiveness is cleanup. Cleaning up the kitchen creates space for the next meal to be made. Cleaning up the barn prepares the table to be filled again. To forgive is clean things up so something new can happen. If life is distilled to reward and consequence, it comes to a screeching halt. Forgiveness doesn't erase all the consequences, any more than cleaning a kitchen makes it look as if it has never been used. Forgiving is not forgetting. Somethings need to be remembered, even when they are difficult or damaging. But we can cleanup and move on.

In restaurant kitchens, everything that goes in the refrigerator is labeled and dated so whoever walks in can see what's there and how long it has been sitting around. One of the purposes of the practice is to avoid using things that are spoiled. It's no fun to open a container and find an unintentional biology project. Cleaning up every night means you don't have to come into the kitchen and play *What's That Smell?* every morning.

When Ginger and I married, we agreed we would not go to bed angry. We had learned the idea from someone else, and it made sense, particularly for someone like me who didn't grow up learning how to effectively express my anger. The power of the practice is that we can trust that whatever anger we encounter, or feel, is tied to the present and not something left in the back of our emotional refrigerator. To be honest and forthright with one another about our feelings is to cleanup on a daily basis.

In baseball, batting cleanup means being fourth in the rotation. The logic is that the first three batters will get on base, so you want your best hitter to be next because they can hit a grand slam home run and cleanup the bases. Instead of it being the denouement of an evening, it is the big event. It doesn't happen every day. Other than the first inning of a game, you can't count on the clean-up hitter batting fourth, not to mention the first three getting on base. In a hundred-and-sixty-two-game season, the number-four batter will hit anywhere between thirty and fifty home runs on average, with only a few offering the chance for a grand slam. For that matter, if they even get a hit one out of every three times they come to the plate, they are excelling. But even with all that might or might not happen, they are designated as cleanup. More often, the one who comes to bat with the bases loaded is not the one batting fourth in the lineup, yet in that moment it is their job to try to clear the bases, even though they may not be the one with the recognized skills. All that is asked is that they do the best they can.

...just beyond the arguing,

there is a long table of companionship

set and waiting for us to sit down.

The only way those on base get to come home is for someone to bat cleanup. The only way for the kitchen to be ready for the lunch shift is for those already tired from a long night of cooking to cleanup. The only way life is more than a series of short painful scenes is for someone to forgive—to cleanup.

The best way to finish an evening at the table is to cleanup together and galvanize the memory.

EPILOGUE:
A GOD WHO GROWS UP

FAITH, LIKE EVERYTHING ELSE IN OUR LIVES, is not static. Because we grow and change, our metaphors must do the same; they are only as powerful as they are relevant.

I think about the metaphors I used to describe my faith twenty or thirty years ago, and I see some I have left behind because God is not the same to me as God was then. One I have carried with me comes from one of the *Chronicles of Narnia*. The children had returned to Narnia for a second time, and Lucy saw Aslan, the lion, and ran to meet him:

> 'Aslan, Aslan. Dear Aslan,' sobbed Lucy. 'At last.'
>
> The great beast rolled over on his side so that Lucy fell, half sitting and half lying between his front paws. He bent forward and just touched her nose with his tongue. His warm breath came

all round her. She gazed up into the large wise face.

'Welcome, child,' he said.

'Aslan,' said Lucy, 'you're bigger.'

'That is because you are older, little one,' answered he.

'Not because you are?'

'I am not. But every year you grow, you will find me bigger.'

To imagine that God grows up with us may seem like an odd image, but it gives me a way to think about how our relationships with God change. And how God changes.

I grew up being told that God never changes. I find deep comfort and courage in trusting that the love of God is indefatigable. But if God is unchanging, then why is growth so central to those of us who are created in God's image? Look at the way a musician's catalog changes from their first record to their last. Look at the way a cook grows in their technique and knowledge of ingredients. Look at the way a writer grows deeper into what they have to say and how they learn to say it. Look at the way we live in our grief and how we grow. I find meaning in paraphrasing the chorus of "Great Is Thy Faithfulness," and singing, "Mourning by mourning, new mercies I see."

For me, one of the sadnesses of aging is seeing people who once had a vibrant faith leave it behind as if it only mattered for the season of their youth. For whatever reason, God did not grow up with them. I have rewritten that sentence a number of times because I am fearful of conveying a tone of judgment rather than communicating my grief.

A century ago, Spanish philosopher Miguel de Unamuno wrote, "We all lack something, only some of us feel it and others do not," which might be another way of saying what I am trying to communicate. He continues, "And I am convinced that we should solve many things if we all went out into the streets and uncovered our griefs, which perhaps would prove to be one sole common grief, and joined together in beweeping them and crying aloud to the heavens and calling for God."

I said early that over the past several years, I had learned to read the Bible as a collection of grief stories. Grief asks us grow up. We are shaped by our sorrows, and we are connected by them, should we choose to grow up with our grief. One of the ways to look at history is to think of it as a story about the world growing up. The same might be said for countries and institutions. As a nation, we had to grow up to see the evils of slavery. We had to grow up to give women the right to vote. We had to grow up to desegregate our schools. All of that growth had to do with coming to terms with grief. For white people—white men, in particular—it has meant coming to terms with the pain and grief we have caused, and growing beyond our childish sense of privilege. Obviously, we still have a lot of growing up to do. These days, it seems to me that we are a petulant adolescent nation, demanding our unconditional independence and acting as though life has few consequences.

Irenaeus imagined Adam and Eve were created as children and their eating of the fruit of the Tree of the Knowledge of Good and Evil was them trying to grow up too fast. The story of creation itself is, at least in part, a story of God growing alongside what God brought into being. That dynamic continues through the Hebrew scripture. For example, God wondered aloud whether to tell Abraham of the planned destruction of Sodom. When Abraham found out, he bargained with God to save the cities if he could find fifty; no, forty; no, thirty; no, twenty; no, ten; hey—how about five good people. After the flood, God promised Noah not to flood the world again. The Incarnation of Jesus gave God experiential knowledge not only of what it means to be human, but what it means to be marginalized. And executed.

God's faithfulness is unwavering. God's attentiveness to creation is unflinching. But God is not immutable. Maybe a better way to say it is the issue is moot because we don't know all of who God is, so we keep finding more—if we keep looking.

Which brings us back to where I started: we can't discover new things about God any more than Columbus discovered this land. God is already here. Or there. Or in between. Brian Wren wrote a hymn titled "Bring Many Names," that names strong *mother God; warm father God; old, aching God; young, growing God*; and *great, living God.*

As we grow, God grows up with us. As we grieve, God grieves with us, mourning by mourning.

For one of my father's birthdays, I channeled my inner Dr. Seuss and wrote him a poem titled "The Skin You're In." It started with these words:

You come into this world and they give you a name,
as though you are going to stay the same.
And every day from there on in,
you're the one living inside your skin.

The problem, you see, is you start to grow and,
so your bones don't start to show,
your skin will sluff and stretch in size
so folks can continue to recognize

Just who you are, though long since gone
is the kid in the cradle, with the sock hat on,
who looked pretty ugly, like most babies do,
and from Day One was considered you.

The seed of the idea came from science class in junior high (maybe?), when we learned that our skin dies and replaces itself. Though we think we are the same people our whole lives, we are actually a succession of regenerative parts that adapt to our world and deal with losses. We grow up, we grow new skin, we grow new ideas, we grow up in love. I ended my poem with these words:

> *So here's to the memories that make up your years,*
> *here's to the laughter, the love, and the tears,*
> *here's to the things your death can't erase:*
> *to forgiveness, to thanks, to hope, and to grace.*
>
> *Here's to the journey that you gave your best,*
> *and the sadness and joy, knowing you are at rest.*
> *After eighty-five years, look at who you have been:*
> *Dad, you were the best you in the skin you were in.*

One way to think about this book is I have tried to show how God has grown up with me. I did not always know how to talk to my father or my mother. I did not always choose relationship over doctrine. I have had to learn how my assumptions have blinded me. I have had to grow into the understanding that a deeper awareness of others awakens my heart to new things. I have had to learn to keep quiet. I have had to learn to listen. I am learning, again, how to hear. And from inside the skin I'm in, I keep learning over and over that we are not alone.

We are made for each other by a God who is love, no matter the metaphor.

ACKNOWLEDGEMENTS

BECAUSE THIS BOOK TOOK SO LONG TO WRITE, I have a number of people to thank for the conversations, texts, and email messages that helped shape these pages. Though this list is far from exhaustive, my thanks to Doug Addington, Claudia Fulshaw, Leon Grodski de Barerra, Patty Clark, Nathan Brown, Peter Palumbo, and Laura Conte.

Julie Fitzpatrick, Terry Allebaugh, Burt Burleson, Hugh Hollowell, and Joy Jordan-Lake read an early draft of this manuscript and provided specific feedback that made it a better book.

Ginger, my wife, read the manuscript at every stage and helped shape it in more ways than I can articulate.

My editor at Light Messages, Elizabeth Turnbull, has offered patience, insight, wisdom, and encouragement all along the way—and it has been a long way. I have not only learned a lot about my writing from her, but also a great deal about how I help other writers in my job as an editor.

My journey in grief has taught me a great deal about what it means to be family. Even though we live in four different states and finding time together is difficult, 1 am grateful that the Cunningham clan—Ginger, Miller, Ben, Jenny, Marissa, and Scott—let me keep telling stories about them.

As for the family that 1 live with, 1 am grateful for Rachel's willingness to tiptoe around the dining room when she thinks 1 am writing, and for offering unfettered encouragement. My deepest love and gratitude go to Ginger, the love of my life. Beyond reading my words, she was written her words of hope and love indelibly on my heart.

REFERENCES

Because I write in conversations with other authors, so to speak, quotations and allusions to other works are scattered throughout this book. I didn't want to fill up the pages with footnotes, but I do want to give credit to those who helped me get my thoughts down on paper by sharing theirs. I hope you will find enough information in what follows to track down references and start conversations of your own.

Berger, John, *And Our Faces, My Heart, Brief as Photos,* New York: Vintage Books, 1991.

Berger, John, *From A to X: A Story in Letters,* New York: Verso Books, 2008.

Berger, John, *In the Shape of a Pocket*, New York: Pantheon Books, 2001

Chimurata, M., *Outside Color: Perpetual Science and the Puzzle of Color in Philosophy*. Cambridge, Massachusetts: MIT Press, 2017.

David Steindl-Rass, "Want to be Happy? Be Grateful," TED, 2013 https://www.ted.com/talks/david_steindl_rast_want_to_be_happy_be_grateful?.

Dawn, Maggi, *The Accidental Pilgrim: New Journeys on Ancient Pathways.* London: Hodder & Stoughton, 2011.

Doyle, Brian, *The Kind of Brave You Wanted to Be: Prose Prayers and Cheerful Chants Against the Dark,* Collegeville, Minnesota: Liturgical Press, 2016.

Gallagher, Nora, *Things Seen and Unseen: A Year Lived in Faith,* New York: Vintage Books, 2007.

King, Stephen, *Different Seasons: Four Novellas,* New York: Pocket Books, 2017.

L'Engle, Madeleine, *Walking on Water: Reflections on Faith and Art,* Wheaton, Illinois: Shaw Books, 2000.

Lewis, C.S., *Prince Caspian: The Return to Narnia, The Chronicles of Narnia,* New York: Harper Collins, 1994.

Moran, Joe, *First You Write a Sentence: The Elements of Reading, Writing...and Life,* New York: New York, Penguin Books, 2019.

Nepo, Mark, *Seven Thousand Ways to Listen: Staying Close to What Is Sacred,* New York: Atria Books, 2007.

Peck, Scott M., *The Road Less Traveled: A New Psychology of Love, Traditional Values and Spiritual Growth,* New York: Simon & Schuster, 1978.

Richard Brody, "Cinephile Follies," *The New Yorker,* August 18, 2011, https://www.newyorker.com/culture/richard-brody/cinephile-follies.

Salinger, J.D., *The Catcher in the Ry,.* New York: Bantam Books, 1979.

Solnit, Rebecca, *Hope in the Dark: Untold Histories, Wild Possibilities*, Chicago: Haymarket Books, 2016.

Solomon, Andrew, *The Noonday Demon: An Atlas of Depression*, London: Chatto and Windus, 2001.

Stavlund, Mike, *A Force of Will: The Reshaping of Faith in a Year of Grief*, Grand Rapids: Baker Books, 2013.

"Talk: Heisenberg's Uncertainty Principle/Uncertainty Sandbox," Wikipedia, Last updated April 25, 2013, https://simple.wikipedia.org/wiki/Talk%3AHeisenberg%27s_uncertainty_principle%2FUncertainty_sandbox.

This is Us, Season 2, Episode 3, October 10, 2017, https://www.nbc.com/this-is-us/video/deja-vu/3596747.

Thurman, Howard, *Deep is the Hunger*, Richmond, Indiana: Friends United Press, 1978.

Unamuno, de Miguel, *A Tragic Sense of Life*, Independently published, 2001.

ABOUT THE AUTHOR

MILTON BRASHER-CUNNINGHAM was born in Texas, grew up in Africa, and has spent the last thirty years in New England and North Carolina. He is an ordained minister in the United Church of Christ, and has worked as a high school English teacher, a professional chef, a trainer for Apple, and is now an editor. He is the author of three books, *Keeping the Feast: Metaphors for the Meal*, *This Must Be the Place: Reflections on Home*, and his latest, *The Color of Together*.

He loves the Boston Red Sox, his mini Schnauzers, handmade music, and feeding people. He lives in Guilford, Connecticut, with Ginger, his wife, and their three Schnauzers. He writes regularly at www.donteatalone.com.